Chris Toombs began his career in Industry and moved into the public sector with Defence, Health, Education and Local Government. He gained experience in Engineering, Design, Management and Law and qualified with a DMS, LLB(Hons), BSc(Hons), CertEd and FRSA. His interests include collecting, restoration, world travel, photography, and writing. Recently retired, he hopes to move to the coast with his partner.

RECYCLING FOR PLEASURE AND PROFIT

Chris Toombs

RECYCLING FOR PLEASURE AND PROFIT

AUSTIN MACAULEY
PUBLISHERS LTD.

A CIP catalogue record for this title is available from the British Library.

ISBN 978 1 84963 335 2

www.austinmacauley.com

First Published (2013)
Austin Macauley Publishers Ltd.
25 Canada Square
Canary Wharf
London
E14 5LB

Printed and Bound in Great Britain

Acknowledgments

I would like to acknowledge Christine, my partner, as my proof reader and general sounding board for ideas.

INTRODUCTION

This book gives examples of the repair, restoration and/or adaption of everyday objects and collectables that might otherwise go to the rubbish tip. It is hoped that this will inspire the reader. The items included in my book are (in the main) otherwise unsaleable bargains because they need repair, care and attention and are targeted at the amateur/would-be crafts person to keep the costs low and affordable. These goods bought and (when satisfactorily) restored cheaply, can now be treasured and used in the home or can potentially be redirected to a new market and sold on at a profit.

Chris Toombs DMS LLB BSc CertEd FRSA

PREFACE

We may all be aware of examples in our consumer society where the "built in" obsolescence especially in high tech products that we buy leads us to take them to the rubbish tip, perhaps only a year or two after purchase. There may not be anything broken but a change in technology or new requirements may be a reason for this. This is truly regrettable in terms of the wastefulness of resources, and the feeling that our hard earned money could have been better spent. Of course there may be some readers that are able to upgrade these products and this is admirable, but the sentiment remains the same.

However, this book focuses more on the low tech items that could be broken for parts or need some attention that we may find at car boot sales, jumble sales, charity shops, second hand/flea markets, antiques/collectors' fairs/auctions, eBay and even the council rubbish tip. My experience is that a damaged or obsolete item from these sources will be close to the disposal/recycling stage in its life. A degree of practical skills, enthusiasm and some basic tools are required by the reader who may wish to undertake similar projects. Also, this book may be similarly of interest to skilled readers with possibly professional tools who might wish to take on bigger and more complex projects. This book is not intended as a guide to antiques or craft skills per se.

The adaption of existing goods and materials for other/special uses is also a challenge. Just as an inventor finds and adapts designs to improve them, the use of lateral thought to solve a problem in an existing project can be most rewarding.

Overall, the idea of "adding value" to existing materials/goods is as sound as the idea of recycling materials in a wasteful society. Most second hand goods tend to sell for perhaps a quarter to a third of the new price depending on age and condition, which makes them affordable. The cost of materials and the parts required for a restoration must be considered as it can outweigh any savings. Materials from damaged goods may also be broken and re-used for other purposes. In addition to this VAT will add another 20% to the shop price which further supports this argument. But the best reason that I have found for the restoration goods is the satisfaction achieved by the finished results of my hard work. Occasionally, when I have sold on a restored item that I no longer need or have room for, I have also made a profit which is a reward in itself and may fund a new project.

INDEX

Chapter 1

RECYCLING IN CONTEXT

Recycling from the rubbish tip has now become a well-established industry with electricity being supplied to the national grid from general waste which is incinerated. Also a whole business of separating used metals, plastics and paper exists to sell these recycled materials back to industry for manufacturing. A flaw in this system could be the dependence on economies of scale in mass production, which can often only be satisfied with new and bigger factories and production processes that may require more energy, consume more materials and produce more pollution. This may not be sustainable as more resources are required and more waste is produced. My examples of restored and recycled goods could help to take away some of this demand for increased production which may encourage built in obsolescence in a "throw away society".

The idea of "make do and mend" or in terms of this book is a case of "repair, adapt and restore" which allows recycling in the main without the need for large scale manufacturing processes, new land sites and more pollution, rather than calling more for craft skills with the use of hand tools.

Strangely enough the austerity years following the last war where it was not unusual for example, to take a suit apart, turn it inside out and then re-sew it together again so that unworn surfaces of the material gave the suit a new look. Further to this a number of DIY magazines at the time such as practical mechanics focused on how to build various domestic appliances that were either not available in the stores or that would be prohibitively expensive.

In the start of the 1990's economic up-wave I witnessed an east London car boot sale supported for the poor by the local council in their grounds, that in a very short space of time turned into an antique and collectors market with prices to match. The council soon pulled the plug on this.

Today, the difference between the post war "make do and mend" austerity is that the tools and materials (recycled) for doing restoration work have never been cheaper. These tools are no longer made of Sheffield steel (unless old recycled ones) and are often of poorer quality, and recycled materials have never been more abundant. And most importantly, with increased leisure time nowadays (and possible unemployment) we may have the need for useful activities to fill the extra time.

For those people who are only interested in boxed new and unused goods (as unwanted presents), I have on occasions come across these at car boot sales in particular, and for often only a half to a third of the new price these goods can find a new home. This creates a business idea for recycling unwanted presents and I have in the past come across a shop called the "gift exchange".

For some time now our less fortunate, possibly skilled and educated neighbours perhaps from Eastern Europe, some of them here to gain higher paid work, are well aware of the austerity in their own countries and that the massive car boot sales surrounding the big cities such as London that are full of the "treasures" thrown out by wealthy consumers, thankfully not to the rubbish tip and provides a supermarket of bargain goods and any repairs where needed are no problem as someone in the family is likely to be able to carry out repairs.

Not long ago I spoke to some self-sufficiency enthusiasts from Ireland's countryside who visits the UK annually to update their household goods from the boot sales described above. Their "idyllic" lifestyle, living in a rural cottage with no services (so no council tax, no income tax, no insurance premiums, no water rates, and no gas or electricity bills?) but enjoy self-sufficiency instead with wood/peat burning for heating, a well for water, and a generator for electricity. A smallholding and local game provides most of the food. The goods purchased at the boot sales were of course much cheaper than new goods and free of VAT.

The Economics of Recycling

As our economy goes through peaks and troughs with us currently in the early part of the second decade of the 21st century we are in a trough with more job losses on the way, the Euro crisis, possibly more Bank collapses, and more Company bankruptcies show us that the austerity years may not yet be over. The main difference between the post war austerity years is that our expectations may be much higher because of economic growth during the good years with greater spending power and new technology being available.

However, to survive, we need to live within our means whatever our present situation and income is. Most of my examples in this book focus on the affordability of the projects shown. In most cases not much more than "pocket money" is used to grab a bargain. To put this into context I am talking about what might be the cost of one or more packets of cigarettes which I understand can nowadays be about £6. Unfortunately, I accept that the goods available to us at, for example, a car boot sale do not always match up with our requirements at the time and so patience is required. But on a positive note, unlike say ordering the exact goods we would like from the Argos store for example, we do not have to pay a retail price or VAT at a car boot sale or the like.

Indeed this is what is known as a 'long wave economic cycle' following what is about a 15 year 'down-waves' and then by alternating 15 year 'up-waves'. This is made more complex by short wave cycles that are superimposed on this. There is nothing precise about these cycles and economists may disagree on their behaviour and length.

New technology tends to lead the new economic up-waves as from the 1930's for example when coal was replaced by oil as a fuel and so on, up to the 1990's when computerisation and the so called "DotCom Companies" led us into the 21st decade until the bubble burst, possibly leading to our economic current down-wave. Perhaps it will be Hydrogen and Electric power in transport that will lead us into the new Upwave. Certainly it is the gearing up, investment and new jobs for new technology that may give the economy a sufficient boost to rise up again.

Based on Harold MacMillan's statement, as the then Chancellor of the Exchequer in 1957, of "you have never had it so good", our next up-wave is likely to start before 2020. This may be led by changes to sustainable energy supply. However, things are never so precise especially as the everyday short-wave economic cycle is super-imposed upon the long wave.

So what has this got to do with readers? The reason for these economic trends in a nutshell is that to those who are interested it will indicate market behaviour such as how people will spend money and dispose of unwanted goods. It will also dictate rapid price rises and demand for antiques and collectables which is very much a cyclical event and the prices for some items such as brown goods remains low at this time. A slow market in housing sales may also contribute to this.

Supply and demand is an all important economic factor regarding the value of goods and where supply greatly exceeds demand the goods may not be saleable, have little or no value (unless for recycling its raw material or adapting it for another purpose) and it will be disposed of at the rubbish tip. (See marketing further on and market saturation).

But of course when the demand exceeds the supply of particular goods such as a useful or collectable item, the value will also be increased. It is not surprising that this rule very much applies to old goods, especially antiques which over many years could have been damaged, become obsolete, and in some cases broken up for firewood. This also points to the fact that in a new Upwave that goods that previously had little saleability and have since been broken up and disposed of, will be even more scarce in a booming market that follows and have more reason to increase in value.

Adapt to survive!

Many examples have already been given of adaptions to existing goods. The skill here is to think laterally. What has a similar use, appearance, design, or construction? When we are used to thinking along these lines the idea of recycling outdated and obsolete goods becomes much easier.

In industry a similar skill has in the past been made for reducing the stock of components held as spares. This process I believe was called "variety reduction". This was used to break down each item of stock held in categories and where duplicated, the stock holding could be reduced saving on the capital tied up, and reducing the storage space required. Similar components that could be varied slightly to perform a multifunctional role, by using our lateral approach could also be used to reduce stockholding.

This may serve to highlight that even large goods that may not have an immediate use for any other purpose can be broken down into components that can be used elsewhere. As a child I often ran out of small brass nuts and bolts for Meccano and I was able to obtain them from my local Radio and TV repair shop where they covered the workbenches and the floor. I was given them by the handful. They were used to hold components such as valve holders to the radio/TV chassis.

As a final thought, even the veneer and inlay used on old furniture can be stripped off and reused where it is not possible to find a suitable match elsewhere.

Some common adaptions include sewing machine treadle bases with replacement marble tops for garden tables and wash stands with new tops to replace the opening for the jug and bowl for indoor use such as a hall table. These and other items are on my earlier mentioned "what not to buy, list" may be found cheaply and are ideal to be adapted.

Some very attractive oil lamps are stored away unused disposed of because they attract dust and have little use unless there is a power cut. I have come across a very useful 'off the shelf' mains electric adaptor for the standard burner oil lamp which involves the removal of the burner/wick holder unit and the replacement with a similar unit having a bulb holder fitted in place of a wick and a cable to connect to the mains. The cable (in the burner with the white bulb) does not need to be taken internally through the base of the lamp so no holes are made which would destroy the original oil lamp, but instead it is hidden behind the lamp. If a candle bulb is fitted, the glass chimney and outer shade can now be returned and the lamp be used as any normal electric table lamp but will look like a working oil lamp. High efficiency candle bulbs can now be purchased for this purpose, and the wick unit can be carefully stored in case the lamp is to be restored to its original design as an oil lamp.

Many items that are on the what not to buy list (it is not comprehensive) may not unfortunately find a place for the original purpose they were designed for, so they may be in danger of being broken up to save space and are disposed of at the rubbish tip. So this list also offers a great opportunity for these goods which after dismantling into parts/materials can be made into new items with a current day usage.

The skills required

This book is *not* primarily intended to be a step by step guide to do it yourself but what to look out for, what is involved, what the likely expenditures are, what can be found, and what can be achieved with limited resources being hopefully an inspiration for others of a "handy" disposition who like bargain hunting and might wish to have a go for themselves. The potential range of skills, tasks and guidance for restorations depending on one's area of interest are virtually too unlimited to be fully described and explained in one book like this, but it is hoped that the reader will look at one or more examples that I have given and to say, "Yes I think that I could do that task, or would like to try that." The craft skills required for restorations can in the main only be gained by practice and experience. This book will hopefully be of inspiration to the use of some, however basic, handyman skills that you already have, to develop into craft skills through practice, trial and error. Just buying an item that needs a good polish and touch up can be an easy starting point. There are many good books on technique that can be followed depending on your own specialist needs. Also the buying and selling skills required should not be ignored, and possibly by using friends with various restoration skills the same might be achieved with limited craft skills of your own.

However, it is hoped that the range of projects and skills involved in each case will inspire the reader to pick out an area of skills to match their own interest of a particular project. For example a project involving woodwork, or upholstering a seat, or rewiring a lamp might be a good starting point. It is hoped that my examples will give a "taster". Perhaps lathe work and welding will give you the opportunity to select and seek out broken metal objects that can be repaired by welding as a specialism.

Regardless of the craft skills, we all have relevant skills that we use in our everyday life that we may not have even considered. Having a "critical eye" is major skill and for anyone who has made an expensive purchase such as a car for example, we may well have looked along each side of the car from an end view position to look for wavy lines in the panels or dents, possibly showing poor repairs to a crash. We might also observe scratches and or fading to the paintwork. This ability can equally be applied to antiques and collectibles.

Even without technical skills these observations, should we wish to purchase the car, would put us in a good position to bargain over the selling price. Furthermore, by using these skills we would be able to take the car to a car body repair shop and give precise instructions regarding what faults need to be put right. At this stage we do not need to know anything about the tools or techniques required to do the work.

In our context, the car example above could equally relate to a piece of furniture in as much as a wavy surface could indicate warped surfaces, dents and scratches and also fading of the finishes. Further to this we might ask if there has there been any restoration that might hide any damage, are there any cracks or splits, is veneer or inlay missing or blistered, is there woodworm, does the furniture stand level or are there loose joints?

Many successful antique dealers can use similar skills (although they do have a specialist knowledge of antiques) to buy for example a piece of antique furniture at auction, to examine the condition, to have it restored by a specialist, and to resell it at a profit. Of course knowing what you are buying and at what price is a part of a dealer's knowledge and experience, and he would also need to take into account the cost of restoration, and the likely profit margin from the sale. Other books should be referred to to learn about antiques.

In my book the repair and restoration of an item would be carried out by yourself, and you would not necessarily wish to sell on the goods and might wish the well restored item to be a feature of your living room. The cost of the restoration should be considered in the initial price of the goods when buying, and the defects should be used as a bargaining point.

An example here is that it may not be easy to estimate the cost of restoration as with the corner chair (see index). The chair was a gift from a house clearance, but the treatment of woodworm was not straightforward. The chemical treatment for about £5 injected into the wormholes brought activity to a halt. But as the seat was to be re-upholstered the webs and cover would not be likely to hold in a frame honeycombed with the (now treated) woodworm holes. The strength of this frail Edwardian chair was questioned as it might be unsafe to use.

Unfortunately the additional expense of injecting a resin into the worm holes which consolidated the wooden structure of the chair became necessary to make it usable again. This additional treatment cost about £20 before the actual restoration had started. Overall, had I paid for the chair I might not have recovered its potential value following the total cost of restoration. However, I was pleased with the finished chair and I found a niche for it in my house and this made the effort worthwhile.

The Tools and Resources Required

If tools and resources make up your stumbling block to taking on some of the projects of the type that I have shown in this book then there are some alternatives.

Many local colleges such as technical colleges, further education colleges, sixth form colleges, and education academies offer evening classes with the use of tools and facilities, however some contribution to materials may be required. Typically, model engineering classes where you can choose your own project will allow access to a range of tools and equipment. Electrical installation/engineering, carpentry, upholstery, car mechanics and welding classes are also commonly available.

Apart from colleges and educational establishments, typically a number of model engineering clubs/societies and the like exist which have tools and facilities available but an annual fee is expected and the projects chosen may be influenced by competitions with other societies and also exhibitions with work on display being representative of that club or society.

At FE colleges with evening classes in model engineering I have personally witnessed for example, 10 year projects to build a scaled down working model of a traction engine, and students bringing their own toolmakers' cabinets full of tools on a trolley for each class. Welding, brazing and most types of machining are often carried out with these facilities.

To some extent, inventors and those wishing to undertake experimental work, could also be carried out within the scope of the model engineering classes with the approval of the tutor and as long as the college rules are met. But any complex set ups would have to be dismantled after each class and comply with health and safety rules.

For those with scope to work from home a range of tools and equipment may be required depending on the type of work you may wish to carry out. The storage of these tools when not in use might also be a problem.

Should you wish to repair furniture we can see in the picture above a small suitcase filed with a range of veneers to match a variety of finishes. Much of the surrounding equipment and materials relate to replacing damaged veneers, patching them or re-fitting existing loose or damaged veneers. Also, general purpose woodworking tools, equipment and materials, for example, measuring and marking out tools, are essential along with tools such as hammers, chisels, saws, pliers and screwdrivers and materials such as nails and screws.

Most directly relating to veneer is the veneer hammer which is shown resting on the case full of veneers. It has a handle with a head at right angles to it which contains a flat brass blade. When the veneer has been placed onto the glued surface we can use the veneer hammer in a zig-zag motion across the surface to squeeze out excess glue and any trapped air. This will ensure good adhesion and a flat surface.

Clamps of many descriptions, including 'G' clamps are also very important to fixing veneer and general woodwork. By securing solid pieces of wood across the glued veneer with clamps we can assist the glue in drying in place and maintaining a flat finish.

When the veneer is set in place we will need to smooth its surface before we apply the finish. I have a mouse detail sander which is particularly good for small detailed areas. A range of sandpaper grades can be used with this to achieve a fine finish. Wire wool of various grades as well as scrapers can achieve a fine finish.

I show a range of surface finishing products from fillers, stains, bees wax, and varnish. Button polishing is also an option normally for small items, but this requires practice and hard work to achieve good results. Finishing itself can be seen as a specialist area and can require reading about technique and lots of practice.

The picture also shows some miscellaneous items which can be useful to know about. A portable steamer is shown and it is sometimes useful when we need to remove glued items including veneer. The steamer will not only help us to unglue most woodworking joints but also help us strip veneer from a donor piece of furniture where a match cannot be found elsewhere.

Otherwise as with fixing anything, everyday cheap items such as cable ties, 'Gaffa' tape and masking tape can help us.

Ideally a garage, workshop, utility room or spare room is needed for most projects which allows the tools required to be kept in order in one place, and also so that we can layout parts of the project for working on and also to allow for any mess not necessarily to be cleared up at the end of each session.

Above we can see located within a corridor, what was a computer workstation with a metal construction (this was to be disposed of on getting a laptop computer) and was used by myself as a work bench for a period of time when I did not have access to my garage workshop. The small clamp on vice made this bench useful for light work and it made a number of tasks possible for me. The location is also not ideal but it shows what can be done with limited resources.

As we might gather, with more skills and equipment the scope of work that might be tackled will increase and more opportunities will arise. Above we have looked at the resources for wood restoration which may be fairly modest especially if we buy tools as we need them, and also to improvise on occasions.

Upholstery is yet another useful area of work that can overlap with the woodworking side of restoration especially where a frame needs repair. Also some of the tools used for woodwork will reduce the need for similar tools, for example for small upholstery jobs a pin hammer will suffice in place of a tacker's hammer with magnetic head, if we wish to forego the picking up of individual tacks from the mouth to driving them into the seat of the chair or sofa. In general the amount of tools required in upholstery can be minimal.

Staple guns as well as pneumatic staplers might also be used in place of tacking where it does not show. Web stretchers, rippers, regulators and long needles for sewing in springs (and buttons) and so forth can be improvised depending how much we wish to specialise in upholstery.

The larger items may include the trestles on which the chairs or sofas may be placed whilst working on them and of course a working area. Other than this the materials such as web, canvas, calico, wadding, horse hair, braid, springs along with tacks, gimp pins, brass headed pins can all be found at local suppliers' shops.

Another, area of skills and resources to look at is minor electrical repairs and rewiring. It must be warned here that unsafe work here might kill by electrocution or by fire, so shared expertise is strongly advised, such as perhaps having a friend as a qualified electrician to check for safety especially in the safe earthing of all metal appliances. Also an outline knowledge of basic electrical principles is required and these can be read from books.

The bonus here is that the tools and materials required for basic electrical work can be minimal compared with some other trades. Usually a range of small screwdrivers, pliers, snips, wire strippers and insulating tape will be a starting point. Circuit testers, multimeters and earth leakage testers may come later, if required.

We can further extend our range of work and resources by including metalwork. Here, the cost and scope of equipment can be extensive, so I follow on from here with some limited examples of the lathe which is primarily for metalwork. It can also be used for materials such as wood and plastics. Further on we look at welding, the cost of resources being a main consideration with both.

However, as in my earlier references to the austerity years after the last war when it was necessary to make do and mend with what was available. In particular I remember a copy of the Model Engineer magazine in the 1950's featuring on the cover a picture of a living room which asked the reader to "spot the lathe" which was normally housed within the sideboard but could be raised to the top surface ready for use after 7pm each evening.

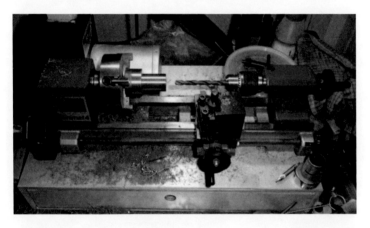

But, we can tailor the projects that we wish to undertake to some extent by the work and equipment required to complete it. So a lathe is not necessarily required for many projects. I own a Unimat 4 metal/wood lathe which is large enough for a range of small work but small enough to put into a Tupperware box in a cupboard, but as in the example above it can used in the living room.

The above Unimat 4 lathe (this can cost about £350) is shown on the small "workbench" shown earlier, placed on a large stainless steel butchers tray to catch cuttings from landing on the carpet. On rare occasions where cuttings and/or cutting oil are thrown out I use a perspex screen to contain them. A small halogen spotlamp is also positioned to light up the cutting tool and the work-piece.

Other skills and equipment may become necessary as with the fruit press where a new threaded stud is fitted. The stud is welded to the base plate of the press as a solution to making the press usable again. I used a cheap arc welder bought for about £40 and with some practice using some scrap steel I was able to produce a strong fixing of the stud. Having invested in the cost of the welder my choice of future projects has now been extended.

I should also point out the special electronic head mounted face shield for arc welding shown in the photo (cost £30) that helps to de-skill welding as it now allows you *to see and position the welding rod* prior to striking the arc which was a big problem in the past.

The equipment for basic welding is shown below, although should you wish to focus on welding projects a MIG (metal inert gas) welder should be considered allowing the joining of not only steel but also aluminium and stainless steel.

Whatever projects we might wish to tackle there are often a small number of repetitive tasks that we might need to undertake time and time again. Sometimes it is this hard graft that is the part of our work that we would prefer to do without. These tasks include the cutting of materials, sanding or smoothing surfaces down and the removal of materials.

To some extent we can make the most of the use of power tools to make our work easier by reducing some of the effort involved. Most commonly we have a modern power drill and possibly a power screwdriver both giving high torque at relatively low speeds. Some power drills combine these functions, and with woodwork in particular using modern chipboard screws we can quickly construct timber frames and structures. For example the chipboard screws used are often 75mm or more long and perhaps only a few 2 to 3mm in diameter requiring no pre-drilling and the best of all the timbers being joined are drawn together giving tight and rigid joints. It would be unusual to revert back to manual screwdrivers.

In the photo above we can see a power saw, power sander and a power file. This is not necessarily a recommendation for a particular brand or product but I can say that for the hobbyist that these or similar items really do make a difference in reducing hard graft and speeding up tasks. However, I would not necessarily recommend these specifically for heavy duty work or for full time trade use. As for the brands available I believe that value for money is not always easy to determine, and that it is not always the price of the power tool itself, but the related cost of consumables to operate it such as spare blades, sanding belts and sanding papers that must also be considered.

However the need for the use of skill, practice and experience is not reduced by the use of the power tools and without adequate care we can easily remove too much material, overshoot our markings and produce scrap. So perhaps we need initially to increase the safety margins of our marking out and measurement.

Planning for future needs and ongoing projects

This relates more to the materials and tools for future needs and projects. It is this crucial practice of carrying a long term 'wish list' in your mind of things that you would like to buy from complete items to parts, materials and tools. This can also include the 'future' antiques and collectables that will become more desirable and rocket in value.

So when you spot an item during your bargain hunt that perhaps you never thought that you could afford, you realise that this is on your long term wish list, and you make a considered decision to acquire it, even though it is not on your immediate shopping list. If you do not think in this way you will be familiar with the scenario of getting home and feeling like kicking yourself as you may never get another chance to buy that special item at the price. The saying 'that all will come to those who wait' may be a truism, but only for those with a wish list!

However, at the other end of the spectrum is the impulse buy which we may later regret. Of course this might relate more to the sum of money paid and not necessarily the choice of goods bought. Also, the condition of the goods bought might later prove to be a disappointment if found to be faulty or not as expected. So we must consider what the top price we would be willing to pay for an item along with realistic thoughts of what condition we can expect for the price we are willing to pay.

Realistically to use a wish list as earlier described we must have some ready cash as 'pocket money' available as things are usually bought on a first come, first served basis. A dealer may accept a reasonable deposit to hold an item to allow you enough time to go to a cash point, but where another buyer is willing to pay the full sum to close a deal, you would be at a disadvantage and could miss out on the opportunity to buy. But many situations and many items of considerable expense are not necessarily as pressurised as this.

Although, I do have many recollections of goods put down after a potential buyer fails to agree a price with the dealer, and another buyer immediately picks up the same item (to their disgust) and offers a slightly higher sum which does secure the goods. The very worst scenario is where two buyers attempt to grab hold of, and make offers on the same item which can only mean that the dealer gets a good deal and not the buyers.

An example of missing out on bargains is illustrated by my past interest in rare cameras. For several weeks in a row a particular dealer at a car boot sale had an unusual camera on display and I asked its price on the last time I saw it. The camera was made of Bakelite and designed unusually with an integral handle and lens and film compartment at the top and I was told that it was reduced to £5. I intended to come back to that stall but I never did. Having looked up the price in a specialist guide possibly, not available to the dealer, the value was shown to be between £150 and £200 and to my regret it was not available the next time I visited the stall. It may have been sold, but it could also have been dumped.

We all know that if we are seeking for a particular item that we are likely to find it if we search specialist antique shops, specialist auctions and on the internet. However, this is not likely to result in finding a bargain and we will probably have to pay a top price. A part of the fun with bargain hunting is that the seller may not be aware or concerned about the true value of the specific item just as the buyer may also not know the true value or be aware of what is a fake, or to find later some damage that was not easy to spot at the time.

It is most unlikely to find that specific item on any particular bargain hunt, but over many years and many outings if you have the item on your wish list it may become a reality. I have over a period of time seen an amazing range of goods and unusual items that I have been able to buy on a one off basis because they were on my mental wish list. Opportunities to buy certain items at a bargain price may never to be repeated.

To illustrate my argument using examples shown in this book I refer firstly to the brass microscope with stereoscopic/binocular

Carl Zeiss lenses which has been a fairly easy, rewarding and much valued restoration. At the time of purchasing this item at the car boot sale some 15 years ago for £10, it was on my long term wish list but not immediately needed and I felt a little angry with myself for spending that sum of money. Although it has only recently been restored I believe that at auction it would not be difficult to realise ten times the sum paid but I am happy to display this item instead.

The Hardy fishing rod was again something that I wished to own but at new prices of about £700 it was unlikely to materialise. Finding this rod at £35 at a car boot sale was something that I could have easily overlooked because it was only if the rod was picked up for examination that the magic make was recognised. Apart from some minor restoration the rod is ready to use.

Having owned an inflatable Avon dinghy for some time which has mainly been used with a small outboard motor, I have wished to use the dinghy with oars to row it, and having made a rudder, to also learn to sail it. Finding a suitable sail to fit my dinghy has been on my wish list for some time and this has become a reality as it has coincided with the need to replace the awning on my caravan. The material from the awning roof will make an ideal sail. However, had I not had the material for a sail on my wish list it might have easily been binned, and I am pleased to be able to recycle this.

As can be seen from the photo above, the rectangular shape in the middle of the material laid out on the ground is approximately 12 feet by 8 feet in size and cut diagonally from corner to corner it will give me possibly 2 sails. The green tails can be cut away as they serve no purpose. However, before any cutting is carried out a mast needs to be found and some careful measurements need to be made.

Possible handles or lens for magnifying glasses (see index) and also small circular marble bases, model brass cannons and lens for the tropical sun dial with noon cannon (see index) and pillars and discs for hour glasses (see index) should all be on our wanted list for car boot sales, flea markets, charity shops and jumble sales.

My choice of Examples

I have selected 54 examples of mainly restorations that I have carried out. Unfortunately not all of my examples include "before and after" pictures as I had carried out many restorations before I had the idea for this book, and some of my earlier works were disposed of many years earlier without any pictures at all and have therefore been excluded from this book. All in all, about a quarter of my examples are with "before and after" photos, and some of which I still find difficult to believe, especially in terms of the desirability of the finished goods compared with the heap of junk that I started with.

The main focus of my examples in this book has been to restore and recycle goods purchased at bargain prices. My sources have in the main been car boot sales, flea markets, charity shops, friends and family and antique fairs.

A minority of examples (as a bi-product of bargain hunting) such as the Coffee Pot (see index) have been chosen for this book purely as a bargain to be re-homed with someone who has that missing part to their collection. This may also help those who have business intentions where profitability is important.

Two examples include affordable kits, the Orrery and the Tellurion (see index) purchased from the internet with both facing the scrap-metal yard, as parts were missing on the former and many lose and unlabelled parts on the latter, to utilise craft and assembly skills to construct desirable completed objects. The main emphasis here, as in my book in general, is the affordability to its readers of things that would otherwise be out of our reach. Certainly I have never before been in a position to splash out many hundred pounds on a brass Orrery or Tellurion, if at all available at that price, but I now own one of each.

My personal taste has been responsible for the bargains and types of goods and projects that I have chosen. I accept that my choice of a bargain might not suit all tastes. However, that with 54 examples it is hoped that a number will appeal to the reader. Also I apologise if my tastes have a male bias and some effort was made on my part to include items for the female collector.

A large number of examples purchased needed some restoration of often a simple nature such as cleaning and polishing, but a minority involved some special tools and skills such as carpentry, upholstery, bench fitting, rewiring, lathe work and welding. So projects can to some extent be chosen to match our skills and equipment.

In many cases the goods purchased had some, often minor missing parts. Normally parts could be substituted from similar equipment, piratised from identical scrap, made to do the job, rarely purchased specifically or a substitute over the counter (when stocked).

Some of my examples are ongoing, or works in progress, such as the Tropical Sundials with Noon Day Cannon (see index) and Magnifying Glasses (see index) where one can only progress with a number of materials or parts that need to be carefully matched together in order to complete each project. This can also mean that our best works may be determined by the materials and parts available at the time. Where better materials and parts allow for a project Mk2, Mk3 projects and so on we might decide to dispose of earlier items and to keep the best of our works at that time.

In a minority of examples I may have mentioned that I have sold on a particular item such as the Dinner Gong (see index), and the Coffee Pot at auction, eBay or elsewhere, although in my case it is usually to de-clutter and to make space for a new project. I also wish to include a business aspect to my book where I mention recycling for pleasure and profit as in the title for my book, it does show that a return on our "investment" of time, effort and materials is possible.

I believe that a variety of my examples here have offered a scope for some research which I feel balances some of the hard graft with interest value. Potentially this makes the restored goods a good talking point to any prospective buyer, or of interest to your friends and family who may value your skills and knowledge.

One example shows recycling at its best, with a "project(s)" of someone else's making. I included this item used by a fisherman on the Sussex coast as a Whelk Pot (see index) This item (one off) was made from used empty 5 gallon plastic container(s) as an excellent example of recycling otherwise non-biodegradable waste, too cumbersome to store for eventual recycling. The fact that we may be able to catch and eat Whelks for tea adds to my attraction to this item.

Chapter 2

THE PRODUCTS

What to Buy?

In the context of this book we are looking for goods that can be recycled, but also we will be seeking to buy for pleasure and profit. It is possible as I have found, that these three facets can often co-exist, in particular it is goods that require care and restoration that are undervalued and are more likely to find their way to the rubbish tip, whilst it is exactly these items that will potentially be the cheapest to buy which makes them more attainable giving more pleasure in gaining something that we want, and it will potentially be more profitable should we wish to sell. Here the term profit need not necessarily relate to the resale value should we wish to sell the goods, but also as an asset that we may wish to keep.

Quite often when we need to purchase an item through the normal retail stores we are surprised at how much they cost. Perhaps we may feel that we have an expensive taste or that we only seem to like goods that are in great demand, and more importantly that everyone else seems to want. If we use these same desires when we are looking for bargains it is also possible that that we can see a heap of junk through the eyes of someone who can restore it to a desirable condition that others will also wish they owned. The type of goods that we choose to buy will greatly relate to our own tastes as we may go on to keep them, and the examples given in this book very much relate to my own taste but perhaps not to everyone else's. So each reader must seek out their own types of bargain and things they may wish to collect or resell. However, I do know that for some specialist areas of collecting, the examples covered here may be in demand.

We are more likely to get a bargain if the goods that we wish to buy are damaged, have a defect or part missing, or in general are not working. This factor increases our bargaining power in haggling over the price, but at the same time we need to consider the work and materials required in carrying out the repair or restoration. Quite often it is possible to visualise how the job will be undertaken and the finished goods. A common mistake after purchasing the goods, is that the work is bigger or more time consuming than anticipated and is shelved, or that the cost of parts and materials in addition to the purchase price exceeds the value of the same item without damage if bought elsewhere.

Goods purchased with parts missing, which may be defective, and not in working order give us greater bargaining power over its price that will help us to get a bargain. The fruit press (see index) may be an example of this with the missing nut of an unobtainable thread type and size. Here the cost of the replacement part is the main concern, and if not available as with the missing nut, the time and cost of making a replacement part must be considered within the purchase price. Again, we need to visualise what would be involved in making the part and if it is possible to make it without for example specialised mass production industrial processes. In my fruit press example a standard threaded stud with nuts and washers offered a cheap solution but the inexpensive welding machine needed to weld the stud to the press base could be seen as grossly exceeding the cost of repair. I justified this expenditure in my mind as an investment by increasing the scope of future projects that may need to be welded.

Where goods may be obsolete for example, in this case as an oak wood fire screen (not in demand with central heating), its conversion into a stand for a dinner gong became an ideal new use. With the central panel of the screen removed, the base with two barley twist uprights either side and a cross bar it was the right size and shape to support an existing brass gong that was of little use on its own. Again, the bargaining point here is whether the goods have a use or need (or even a decorative value) in today's market, however, the finished item as a dinner gong has now become desirable as a decorative item, possibly with some use value, later sold at auction.

Alternatively, as above we may also see the obsolete goods purely as parts possibly for use perhaps as timber to be made into an up-to-date usable form for example, and the same rule applies.

Certainly, anything that is undervalued is a good starting point when looking for a bargain. An example of this is the tripod used with the telescope as shown further on in this book. The (surveyor's) tripod had been covered in a dark green paint and although it was exactly what I needed for the telescope, various brass fittings on it were covered. Although I was going to buy the tripod anyway, it was only later that I was able to scrape the paint away to reveal these brass fittings. Had the polished brass been shown it could have perhaps fetched ten times it value, especially at somewhere like London's Portobello Antiques Market.

The goods may also be undervalued because of the ignorance of the seller in that they have not been properly recognised or classified. This should not be a problem to us if the seller is happy with the price, but in case they are aware of some damage that we have not yet found, we should examine the goods closely. Funnily enough, I have bought goods from a woman at giveaway prices purely because as I later discovered, they belonged her ex-husband and she just wanted to clear all traces of him.

General cyclical trends may bring prices down and in a recession the prices given in the Millers Guides for collectables may appear as fiction, certainly when you are trying to sell them. This may of course be the right time with low prices to buy collectables if you wish to build collections regardless of trends, or to deal in them to stock up now before an upturn in the market.

The cyclical trends may also exist in terms of mainly large freestanding brown goods like wardrobes, cupboards, sideboards, tables and desks. This is more complex to understand as retired baby-boomers may wish to downsize, and new house owners with the high price of land and property are tending to buy smaller properties. This may be contrasted by times of economic boom when City dealers splash out their bonuses and upwardly mobile people may wish to trade up to a bigger property, and fill them with large pieces of furniture.

Goods such as silver, brass and copper items also seem to be in a cycle, and I understand that the current position is that less people wish to spend time and effort on polishing these goods. This may also be linked to the property market which is currently down, but I am sure that the vision of the country cottage with brasses around a cosy fireside has not died, nor indeed the grand town house with silver tea services and on the dinner table silver candelabras and cutlery.

This raises the question of buying specialist items which may not be at all in demand (and appear to be worth little) unless we seek out the market for those specialist goods. So should we buy cheaply at a general market we may be able sell at a higher price at a specialist auction such as eBay.

What Not to Buy or Sell?

Perhaps the most compelling urge to buy is when we like a particular item which we may wish keep rather than sell. Perhaps this chapter should not necessarily deflect us from buying what we like. However, if we spend a significant sum of money on an item we might have difficulty in selling it on, and recovering our money in the future. The idea of the cyclical demand for certain types of goods has been covered and these demands are unpredictable. We should only consider buying items on the following list if you like them, have time to wait, have much storage space, and when they are at a rock bottom price and/or are exceptionally good examples. An example of cyclical demand, in retrospect, are telephones from the 1960's to the 1980's which could have been picked up for as little as £1, are now seen at prices from £25 to £80 but many are probably still in storage for release on to the market at the right time.

We previously mentioned goods that require regular cleaning and polishing, goods that have limited use value in modern times, and brown goods that are large and bulky may all loosely come into this category. It should be noted that this might well include some items covered in this book but as in the main I like the items I have bought, they have not necessarily been bought to sell or to make a profit, and I have paid very little for them and any money recovered for them in the future would tend to be a bonus.

It would be interesting to know how many young people who are becoming householders will become interested in old/historic goods, collectables and antiques. To some extent this will be determined by their disposable income, and the type and size of their homes. Many modern homes are not compatible with the design of old things and certainly the smaller properties such as a studio flats have little space for anything other than the most essential and usable items. Some of the Art Nouveau and Arts and

Crafts designs of which William Morris said ''Have nothing in your house that you do not know to be useful, or believe to be beautiful''. Probably the most stylish items that will fit in with many modern homes are the Art Deco designs especially in ceramics, household goods and chrome furniture many fitting in with minimalistic designs. Further to this almost every decade from the 1940's utility style onwards up to the end of the 20th century including Ercol and "G" Plan furniture may offer some distinct and collectable styles for the future that may suit small homes.

It goes without saying that the modern household with electric lighting, central heating, flush toilets and non-smokers have made a tremendous change to our needs. But probably the most significant change has been that the fireplace is often no longer the central feature of our living rooms. However, this does not alter and may drastically affect the quirkiness factor of wanting to own for example, an oil lamp that may only be used very rarely during a power failure!

Individual items not to buy can include the following in basic and general condition but please use your discretion for exceptional items. Alternatively, the following list may present a buying opportunity where the low price is an all important consideration and you are willing to wait for changing trends in demand. So if you wish to buy any of the following, expect big discounts or low prices.

Brass, Copper and Silver Plate

- Brass/Silver plated Candlesticks
- Basic Oil Lamps
- Horse-Brasses
- Bedpan Warmers
- Fire Guards
- Fenders
- Andirons
- Fire Surrounds
- Fire Tools
- Trivets
- Kettles/Pans

- Coal Scuttles
- Fire bellows
- Silver plated tea accessories
- Silver plated kettles/teapots/coffee pots
- Silver plated condiment sets
- Silver plated napkin rings
- Silver plated toast Forks/Racks
- Silver plated Knife Rests
- Silver Plated Fish Knives/Forks/Servers
- Silver Plated Cake/Desert Knives & Forks
- Silver Plated Trays

General Goods

- Some Barometers
- Various kitchenalia
- Wash Stands
- Jugs & Bowls
- Chamber Pots
- Commodes
- Pewter/Ceramic Tankards & Steins
- Glass/Ceramic Beer Jugs
- Some Decanters
- Plaster figures
- Plaster Busts
- Some Biscuit Barrels
- Some Rolling Pins
- Glass/Ceramic Jelly Moulds
- Common Smoking Accessories
- Some Ash Trays
- Ash tray stands
- Some Tobacco Jars
- Large sideboards
- Dressing tables
- Free standing wardrobes
- Chests of drawers
- Blanket chests/Ottomans
- Umbrella Stands

- Hat Stands
- Coat Racks
- Lamp Standards
- Some Book Cases
- Some Tables/Desks
- Old hair dryers
- Some Bakelite collectables
- Some Books
- 78's
- Video Tapes
- Cassette Tapes
- Some common Typewriters
- Some mechanical adding machines
- Some old sewing machines
- 1950's & 1970's Soda Syphons
- Overmantles
- Basic film/plate Cameras

NB: Some exceptional examples only, of the above could be in high demand and have high values.

However, the goods listed above may be at the risk of being dumped as rubbish when in some cases they may be recycled by adaption to more useful purposes, and failing that the materials especially with large old wooden furniture may be useful in their own right to make new or restored goods. Please refer to the above chapter entitled "adapt to survive". For these reasons alone and with a low price these goods could be argued to be what you should buy, but only if these meet with your requirements.

It should be noted that items listed above may well be accepted in general auctions but that it is likely that they may not (all) be accepted into some antique auctions. The reason for refusing goods that may not sell is that the auction house will not make commission on a 'no sale', also large items take up space that might be used to sell more profitable sale items, and the buyer has to be chased up to collect the large goods which in the case of furniture may have to be burned if not collected.

Where to Buy or Sell

Does this look like a car boot sale or an antiques fair? In fact this is the same car boot sale as is shown in the photo further on with bric-a-brac spread out over the ground. The fact is that over many years I have seen an exceptional range of goods for sale and unusual things to see. This also includes a large variety of both legal and illegal goods of all descriptions. Cars, campervans, quad bikes, motorcycles, trailers have also been for sale along with other large items such as fridges and freezers, wardrobes, three piece suites and king-size beds. A part of the fun is discovering what will actually turn up at the next car boot sale.

In the early 1980's at the start of the recession I recall an unfortunate seller at a Whitechapel Old Brewery car boot sale selling off unwanted (not designer wear) clothing from the boot of a Rolls Royce Corniche motor car and I thought to myself, that the takings would not even be likely to even half fill the petrol tank with fuel. At 50p to a £1 an item this would be an unusual business even for a would-be Spiv.

The occasional car boot sale may offer us a surprise in the type of goods that show up which could be something that we have been seeking for many years as spare parts or bits and pieces that we may need to complete a project. These spare parts may even come from an item identical to that which we wish to repair but not in working order, so we can buy it cheaply and then piratised it for the parts that we need.

The above photo is more like the type of car boot sale that we might find some bargains and missing parts, however, let me say that this is the same car boot sale site as the previous photo, but the stalls were not located close to each other.

In my view car boot sales have overshadowed jumble sales, second hand shops, flea markets and to a lesser extent charity shops which are numerous and open all week all year round instead of just one day a week. I will not dwell too much on the others except for the charity shops but we must not ignore the internet and eBay for example. A few recycling shops do exist as in Leyton, East London where a whole range of goods is available including DIY materials such as part used tins of paint. In particular, in the big cities especially in the London suburbs, the car boot sales between spring and autumn are mainly on Saturday and Sunday mornings and can be massive and meet most individual's needs for recycled goods.

Car boot sales tend to cater for sellers who may fall into the following categories, the regular dealers who may be market traders and dealers involved in house or refuse clearance, then the non-dealers who are often elderly householders downsizing, and the younger couples who need to de-clutter and raise some cash. Incidentally, there is a definition of a dealer which relates to how many times a year goods are sold on a particular site. This could have income tax implications so if you are a casual trader, beware.

The dealers may offer the most interesting goods for sale but will usually be the most resistant to haggling for bargains, as regulars they can hold on until future sales. The elderly downsizers may have interesting items but remember the new prices paid and would rather keep them than to sell cheaply, but they may respond to your enthusiasm for items. Finally, young couples who need cash and will usually take reasonable offers, whereas divorcees tend to almost give away any reminders of the ex-husband especially with tools and technical items!

A common ploy used by dealers or very keen buyers (at some car boot sales, jumble sales, and various antique fairs) who are buying at events especially jumble sales where queuing for an opening time and an entrance fee is payable, (not the "dealers preview"), is for a £50 note to be produced by one of a pair of dealers at the front of the queue to pay for two 50p admissions, bringing the entrance to a halt, whilst the other one of the pair has entered and is left to take their pick of any of the best bargains on offer.

The 'early bird' might get the bargains at the car boot sales, but I can say that I have picked up bargains well after the boot sale opens. The former is likely to be true to some extent but this could mean that not all items are put out immediately or that I am the only person up until that point that has recognised the bargain.

Likewise, we might consider whether at a massive boot sale like Dunton in Essex that it would have a better starting point for finding bargains than at the main entrance. I recently explored this idea at a large car boot sale with one main entrance that allowed in cars and pedestrians. Just about everyone started by the gate at the first row of stalls, possibly spending all of their pocket money well before reaching half way and then taking goods back to the car and often leaving before completing the sale. This time I chose to park at the far end of the boot sale and I found far more bargains than if I had, as regularly before when I started by the entrance, where it often appeared that nothing was worth buying.

Charity shops are numerous and in most high streets, and the fact that they tend to be open all week instead of just the one day a week of most car boot sales, flea markets and jumble sales. They are also an important source of recycled goods along with the fact that they also raise money for good causes.

In general, charity shops tend to sell the smaller general second hand goods and may also have branches that only stock the larger goods such as furniture, TV's, and other white goods such as fridges, cookers, freezers and so on. Whereas, some other charities have specialist book shops with also DVD's and CD's. A small number of charity shops have very little in the way of second hand/recycled goods tending to specialise in new products which may be from third world/fair trade countries only, and often have things like birthday and Christmas cards.

The best deals from charity shops tend be found from newly donated goods, or where goods are supplied from a central source on the days when the shop is re-stocked. It is also possible when an item has been left unsold for a period of time (number of days/weeks) to ask the shop manager to accept an offer. The pricing of an item may often be illogical especially when the use or classification of an item is not fully understood and this can be in our favour, although we may have no wish to short change a charity. Finally, certain goods, possibly jewellery or antiques may be put aside for dealers, only.

The frequency of jumble sales is often depending upon where you live, they may not be very regular, or certainly far less frequent than the pre-boot sale years of the mid 1980's which may now be in competition with them.

I have many years of experience of jumble sales which were mainly held in church halls and often used to raise funds for the church. These jumble sales varied very much in terms of the quality of the goods for sale, depending very much on the areas the goods were collected from by the scouts/guides, or on the church locals living in wealthy parishes and their donations. Today, these factors are still likely to be the same although the less frequent seasonal jumble sales may still take place.

I remember a 'fellow' jumble sale bargain hunter in the 1960's whom I believe is the author of the Guide to Second Hand & Antiquarian Bookshops in Britain" and is believed to be an expert having appeared in a TV documentary in the 1990's. From the mid 1960's for several years, I recall him at a number of jumble sales on Saturday afternoons where he bought books and loaded them into the large front basket of his butchers' bike. He then cycled 12 miles from north London to the book specialists in the Charing Cross Road to sell them. In the TV documentary he is said to have purchased houses around London and filled them (floor to ceiling) with rare books, and could charge £100 per hour to track a particular title. So a lesson may be learned from this self-styled career as a rare book expert!

It may be worth mentioning that at the end of a jumble sale where the unsold goods are not stored for the next sale, it is often possible to make an offer to clear, for example, all of the remaining clothes, books, bric-a-brac or all of the stock should you have an outlet for them.

The flea markets during the winter season when the (open air) car boot sales may have ceased, may be worth exploring. In particular, I have knowledge of the east London flea markets such as 'Kingsland Waste' and parts of Camden Passage on Saturdays and Cheshire Street on Sundays.

Out of London some good flea markets include Rochester in Kent and Saffron Walden and Ely. The usual rule is that "the early bird catches the worm" and that we should haggle for the best price. This is where my trolley in a bag is important as it is not usually possible to park next to the market.

Antiques markets around London include places such as Bermondsey on Fridays, Camden Passage in Islington and parts of Camden Lock in Chalk Farm and Portobello Road in west London. There are regular antique collector's fairs at Alexander Palace in north London on Saturdays. Outside of London we should consider the regular antique fairs in Ardingly in Sussex and Newark in Nottinghamshire which are both massive events.

Also at Battlesbridge in Essex there are a number of indoor antique shops and an antique flea market. But it must be said that we must expect to pay much higher prices for goods from these sources.

In addition to the Battlesbridge antiques centre in Essex there are also regular auto jumbles (some for particular makes of car) motorcycle jumbles, and boat jumbles. At each of these jumbles which have an entrance fee it is possible to enjoy the atmosphere and to find some vintage collectables along with some cheap tools and equipment. The boat jumble had a surprising number of nautical collectables/antiques at all prices with some possible restoration projects.

E-bay must be considered as a serious option for buyers and sellers alike. The classification of goods on e-bay may be extremely useful to finding unusual items but it is I believe necessary to register with Pay-Pal to make and receive payments. However, the cost of mailing the goods must be taken into account unless the buyer collects, so this is not my favourite for larger items.

The local rubbish tip should offer some good opportunities for recycling and restoration projects, and this makes good sense especially as it was shown on the BBC news that we will soon officially be able to re-cycle goods from the rubbish tip but I have not heard anything since.

Apart from asking for permission to remove items from the tip (and offering a payment) I do not know how to go about doing this. Unofficially, of course it is possible not only to place goods on the tip, but to pick up items to go back in the car. I think that this action could be technically interpreted as theft, and anything left on the tip becomes the property of the owners of the tip, but it could also be argued that rubbish has no value when the aim was for it to be disposed.

What must also be considered here is that the bin-men and those associated with waste disposal often have a second unofficial job as 'Totters' at flea markets and car boot sales, and I do not think they would willingly allow their second income to be taken away.

Antiques and Collectables

The demand for collectables comes and goes in cycles, and this should be borne in mind by collectors and especially those who are interested in making a quick profit. In particular, the choice of items that we choose to purchase should be strongly influenced by this where we may wish to make a quick turnover of stock and profit. However, this cycle might indicate that for those who are prepared to wait, the low demand/prices indicate that this could also be a good time to buy. My own personal interest is, however, not so much in the selling of goods but more the need for space.

Examples of items that are currently out of favour include those which require regular polishing such as brass kettles, bed warming pans and brass fire surrounds/tools and silver plated goods such as ice buckets, candelabra, drink trays and punch bowls. Brown goods such as large pieces of furniture may be worth more as recycled good quality wood than in their current form. Some other goods that are currently out of demand include plastics, barometers, typewriters, and soda siphons to mention a few. First class examples of all of these may be exceptions to the rule, but they might also require a relatively high outlay in the first place.

Quirky items that have a novelty as well as a use value such as the dinner gong example are often choices that will do well for resale especially at auction. Also items that do not take up too much space may also be favoured where our potential market may include perhaps retired people that have downsized their accommodation, and no longer live in large houses.

Your bargaining power is vastly increased when you purchase an item that the seller does not know what it is or for, as can often be the case when the seller deals in house clearances or deceased's effects. If the object is unidentified it becomes harder for the seller to place a value or establish the usefulness (if it has no purpose who would want it anyway) or need for it, but if you know your stuff you can gain from this. An example of this is the prayer chair which is rare compared to an ordinary chair and may fetch a slight premium because of this. The ballot box example sold as a "box with drawers" may also come into this category because of its use in selecting members of exclusive and secret societies from which the term of being "black balled" may have originated. Conversely, by telling the seller how much you want or need an item for a particular purpose can work against you in terms that you are already "hooked" at that price, or they will expect that others will also value it highly as well.

Another point to consider is that by buying a specialist item at a general sale for a low price, as it is not of any particular interest to most the buyers present, this can then be sold at a premium by targeting specialist buyers or collectors on eBay or at specialist auctions.

Items that now have little use value such as for example an ordinary wooden fire screen at a time when most people have central heating, is likely to be a prime target for the rubbish tip. Such an item although more scarce these days, is subsequently likely to be in little demand and cheap to buy. However, as with dinner gong mentioned above, this is the result of a "marriage" not unusual in the antiques trade, between a fire screen (with panel removed) and a suitable sized gong, and striker. Ethical issues may arise here, as with hidden repairs that may affect the value of the goods and should be declared to the buyer.

It is no secret that for brown goods, it is the smaller items such as a compact desk like a Davenport may be favoured, whereas large sideboards and wardrobes tend to be used for timber or burned. Not long ago, I took a large scotch chest of drawers to auction and luckily it sold for a reasonable price of I believe approximately £80 at the time, but I had been told that if it did not sell it would be burned if not collected within 3 days. Because of this, items such as large good quality sideboards may be scaled down, with sections removed, to make them more compact, more usable, and worth buying.

Further to the size of furniture and the more compact size being favoured there are some other examples. Desks and work stations for example, possibly used with (old) large computers having separate monitors and processing units required considerable storage until modern laptop computers could provide the same level of operating power, and could be used perhaps with the smallest of desks and stored folded. This could now mean a surplus of the larger desks and workstations being no longer required and ready for the tip. I have salvaged a small metal workstation from computer use and now it is a small work bench having a vice fitted on one corner and when required it is ideal to support a small lathe.

Restorations can include rebuilds of broken items such as the art nouveau bust example. This was bought with the upper part of the bust in pieces, and taken away in a cardboard box.

General Goods

Here I refer to items that may be considered as being general goods as opposed to antiques and collectables. However, the range and scope of items within this category is immense. It can only be said that many items within the range covered in this book have similarities and as such may require a similar treatment. Preparing for a new surface on either wood or metal as with the mountain bike frame (see index) as an example both may require rubbing down possibly with wet and dry paper on the frame and with sandpaper on the wooden surface, using finer grades until smooth enough for priming and then painting or varnishing. The transferable skills that are gained from each project will help with ever increasing expertise to be gained.

Mechanical items such as the mountain bike may require a rebuild as a part of the restoration. Here, the whole project could consist of stripping the bike down cleaning (painting and oiling where necessary) and repairing/refitting and/or replacing worn parts with newer or refurbished/repaired parts.

Other skills may become necessary as with the fruit press example where the new threaded stud is fitted. The stud is welded into place to the base plate of the press as what I considered to be solution to the problem of making the press usable again. I used a cheap arc welder bought for about £40 and with some practice using some scrap steel I was able to produce a strong fixing of the stud. Having invested in the cost of the welder it will increase the choice of projects that I can tackle in the future.

Most painting can be carried out with a brush, but the use of aerosol paint can greatly improve results in terms of professional finishes. Again as with the welder this will extend the range and quality of the work that we can tackle.

Chapter 3

HOW TO MAKE A PROFIT?

Although this sounds extremely mercenary it is far better to make a profit as obvious as that appears, than it is to make a loss. Profits are in no way guaranteed as goods may not sell at all, let alone make a loss. If we are to continue with our chosen projects and enterprise we need not only to have a return on our efforts in time, and materials and consumables, but also an incentive to continue with our work.

However, I like many of the objects chosen as examples in this book and I may wish to keep them. In this case the choice of "what to buy" and "what not to buy" is not relevant. But it goes without saying that with a sound purchase at the right price should give us a profit if we wish to sell. This may also be a key factor in recycling goods rather than to scrapping them.

The process of "adding value" to these goods is by the process of restoration and this requires investment in money, time and materials which needs to be recovered out of the profits that we are discussing. As opposed to the "wheeler dealers" who aim to buy cheap and sell high they do very little in the recycling process when the goods may be at the end of their life and ready to be scrapped, unless it is sold on to a restorer.

To sell our goods for the best profit we need to market them. As with any goods the rules of marketing apply and this will be covered later in this section. These rules include where we sell, to whom we aim to sell , the price that we ask and how we promote the goods. If we get these wrong we may not be able to sell our goods at any price.

Adding Value

One of the key features of this book on 'recycling for pleasure and profit' is that the goods that we salvage from the tip are to some extent restored for normal use. Because of the condition of the goods purchased we may have spent very little money to buy it, and the time, work and material input used to restore it to normal condition can be described in terms of the added value of the finished goods.

The saleability of the finished goods should now have increased along with the sale price achieved if resold. This asking price should firstly recover the original price paid, the time, work and materials spent on the restoration, and any special factors such as the 'USP' (unique selling point). Any excess will represent a profit, all of which make up the selling price.

The idea of adding value, especially in the industrial sense as an input of labour to process raw materials can be considered as true wealth creation as opposed to the service industries which tend to move around existing resources. In our case we are to some extent recycling existing materials that might otherwise be destined for a rubbish infill site thus saving a waste of what may become scarce resources, and saving the energy and CO_2 gases required to produce the same goods as a new item.

It might also be said that just to find a new and useful application for an object that is obsolete in its old role, especially if the buyer is convinced of this, is in effect adding value. Although in many applications some modifications will be necessary and this to some extent this also contributes to recycling.

The Best Situations to Buy or Sell

This may depend on the type of goods involved, the place that we have decided to market our goods, the time of the year, weather conditions, any seasonal aspects affecting sales, and economic environments (already covered in economics of recycling).

In general terms as a seller we require a high level of 'footfall' wherever we trade. Sometimes this is almost guaranteed where the location is linked to other types of trading such as being close to a high street, bus/train depots, retail/industrial parks and anywhere that has a busy cut through to other sites. One place that has a massive and extremely busy market throughout the year (even though it is not close to or linked as above) is on an airfield that is hard standing, with a regular car boot sale that gives the market access via the massive car parking areas. So both the market and the boot sale gain in footfall on entering or leaving the market as the buyers walk past the car boot stalls to get to their cars. It has been proved that linked trading does overall, bring gains to all concerned even if it is thought that the competitors will benefit more, as the worst scenario is where too few spenders are attracted to an area.

The place that we have decided to market our goods will have an effect on how we buy or sell our goods. Certainly for buying at places such as antique markets, flea markets, car boot sales and the like it is well accepted that the 'early bird catches the worm'. The choice and quality and quantity of goods will be greater and this is favoured by dealers, so much so that especially in the winter, torches and head lights are used in the early hours of the morning to assist in the search. But for sellers they may expect dealers to show interest and put up prices accordingly, knowing that they may have perhaps half a day ahead to make a deal and refuse to be pressured into a sale. Sometimes, the early buyer may turn out to be the only serious buyer for certain goods that might otherwise be difficult to sell.

However, being a "late bird" can also have some advantages in that when, for example, the stalls are being closed it is not unusual for the sellers to have some idea of how good or bad takings have been and whether the clearing of one or more items might be important, especially for breakable and bulky items which take up storage space at home. This situation can create good bargaining opportunities for both parties.

Weather conditions can benefit or also be disastrous for buyers and sellers. A typical scenario that is good for buyers is where a flea market or car boot sale for example, starts early in fine weather conditions so that a large number of sellers set up stalls, but quickly black clouds come over and it buckets down with rain. The number of buyers now setting out to these sales are drastically reduced, so for the buyers that do brave the weather, even after the rain stops, they may well find more bargains and have a greater bargaining power, especially if the weather remains unsettled. However, sellers who had not brought tarpaulins to protect their stock may end up throwing away soggy books, clothing and other soft goods. Unfortunately, the entry fee to a flea market/car boot sale is not normally refundable so many stallholders stay hoping for a recovery.

Seasonal conditions in general terms can benefit both buyers and sellers. We expect caterers to benefit by selling cold foods in the summer and hot foods in the winter but what else should be considered? In general, holiday periods also create opportunities in terms of warm and/or cool clothing, but festive times such as Christmas and Easter tend to make people more generous in terms of giving presents and spending money if only for a short period of time, giving a boost to most forms of selling. In particular, activity on the internet selling of goods such as DVD's, CD's, Videos; any possible forms of presents can increase drastically.

Higher taxes or VAT, and/or high inflation may favour the sellers of used goods which are very likely to be less sensitive to price changes. However, a recession may well tighten spending all around and not just for new goods. Also, seasonal and ongoing sales may attract buyers to buy new goods especially where discounts of 50% or more off is expected rather than to buy old/used goods at similar prices.

In times of economic hardship the idea of collecting and collectable goods becomes less important to many people and essential and immediate goods/needs have to be recognised and dealt with. This could either mean for some sellers that changing stock is necessary or selling less collectables and at a lower price is a likely outcome. But of course the brave buyer of collectables may do well to buy cheaply but find there are far less sellers to buy from.

Marketing our goods

The four "P's" applied here are the price, the product, the promotion and the place. Most of the things that can go wrong in the process of selling our goods may relate to any one or more of the 4 P's. Each of the 4 P's may be tinkered with to achieve the best results. Probably the best known of the P's is the price for example, as in supermarkets for food with the "lost leaders" and at the petrol station with 1p a litre off fuel may make us drive to another garage for a better deal.

For price sensitivity a recent example was at (an up to 50%) closing down sale of a well-known DIY store where the car park for the last 6 months had been almost empty, even at weekends with corresponding low sales. At the start of the sale the car park was full as was the store. Inside the discounts were mainly 20%, but the prices of the goods were also upped by about the same amount and buyers like myself were not fooled and left empty handed, as quickly as they had arrived. So quite simply we do not buy if the price is not right.

Price elasticity is also a factor to be considered, where if we were to plot a graph of sales achieved against the price required, it will show that as we increase our price the number of sales will proportionately be reduced. I have noticed at one extreme that where a stall consists of mainly high priced, small items such as watches and jewellery and the seller is reluctant to sell cheap, that when the occasional sales are made at high prices it can still be a worthwhile business to the seller. However, with perhaps large, low priced goods, the opposite scenario might well be the case and needs to be avoided.

If the products that we have chosen to buy or sell loosely comes under the heading of antiques and collectables then the general area may be covered in my section on "what to buy", and "what not to buy", to some extent. But we do need to know our product in detail, especially as we need to target those who may be interested in collecting these goods. These goods are often sub-divided into many specialist areas such as "scientific instruments" for example.

The promotion may include a number of things but normally it is more about what is on offer, for example, the chairs are £25 each, or £80 for all 4, the table for £40, or 4 chairs with the table for £100. Of course some haggling may determine the outcome but we need to offer an attractive package at the outset that promotes what we want to sell, with perhaps an incentive to sell the table and chairs as a set.

Further to promoting your goods and pricing I have found that when buying in bulk, for example a box of mainly broken tin steam toys I was amazed at buying a box of at least half a dozen items for about £20. When I sold them on, I found that by splitting them up that I could ask for up to £20 for each item. So how we combine or split up goods is important to getting the best return on our money. I found that it is not a good idea to throw in extra piece when the demand is high as a part of the deal. So to this end, I only put on the table one piece at a time even when the same person might have purchased the whole lot (at a large discount).

Each item may have a unique selling point (USP) and this may include age, rarity, condition, quality and maker. These points can be used to justify your price and why the buyer should buy your goods as opposed to similar goods elsewhere. The promotion also includes the display and presentation of our goods; for example, on a stall we can use perhaps blue or green velvet throws over the table tops so that the goods appear as special and not just bric-a-brac. Glass display boxes and cabinets further enhance the goods on display as being special and valuable. By being asked by the seller for a closer look and my removing it from the cabinet I believe showed a more serious interest, and a greater chance of buying the goods.

The place that we offer our goods for sale these days may include the internet, as with e-bay for example. Most importantly, the place must be where our potential buyers will be seeking to buy the type of goods that we are selling. The interesting thing here is that if we wish to sell for example a 'humidity recorder' we are more likely to get the right price if we target the scientific instruments section of e-bay, or at an auction for scientific instruments, rather than a general market place. In fact it can be a good deal to buy specialist goods low at a general market and then to sell them high at a specialist market where there are more potentially interested buyers to compete with each other.

As we can see from the examples given above juggling one or more of the 4 P's may be necessary for each situation, and that the promotion, and the price achievable, may vary from place to place.

The rules of economics should also be borne in mind in the case of supply and demand. A high level of supply can create market saturation and a low sale price, whilst a high demand may create a scarcity and a high price for a specific good.

Another rule that I have found is that in boom times when there is much money around it is easier in general terms to make a profit when people will buy on a "whim". In the current recession it is much harder to make a sale on someone's "whim" and if so it is likely to be the exception than the rule. But it should be easier to sell our recycled goods at a profit as we should have been able to buy them at rock bottom prices and then sell at a competitive price.

Market research is important and information can be gained purely by observation. If we are selling from say a market stall for example, we should observe what goods are looked at and perhaps handled, and the goods that are consistently ignored. We can also observe the same goods that remain unsold and are returned to the same boot sale week after week.

Also, at auction we may see that consistently some goods do not sell, whereas other items always sell, and fetch a good price. We can then perhaps form our own list of "what not to buy, or sell" list, and who are the potential buyers to be targeted.

Although the term 'saturation' is used mainly for new mass produced goods flooding on to the market, the principle still holds true for any goods that we may wish to buy or sell as described in this book, although to a lesser extent. The economic rule of 'supply and demand' comes in here, and for the buyer with even only one similar good for sale in a market place we would be wise to shop around for the best deal/price. As a seller we might wish to know what our competitors' asking price is, so that we might adjust our price to be more competitive. In the extreme, for example, perhaps with reproduction collectables of a particular type flooding the market, as a buyer we may be put off buying the goods 'as you can get them anywhere'; and for the seller either the lower price required to gain interest or disinterest will be driven to a point where 'we no longer wish to trade' and will prefer to take the goods home.

As mentioned earlier under "The Best Situations to Buy or Sell", in general terms as a seller we require a high level of 'footfall' wherever we trade. Sometimes this is almost guaranteed where the location is linked to other types of trading such as being close to a high street, bus/train depots, retail/industrial parks and anywhere that has a busy cut through to other sites. One place that has a massive and extremely busy market throughout the year (even though it is not close to or linked as above) is on an airfield that is hard standing, with a regular car boot sale that gives the market access via the massive car parking areas. So both the market and the boot sale gain in footfall on entering or leaving the market as the buyers walk past the car boot stalls to get to their cars.

It has been proved that linked trading does overall, bring gains to all concerned even if it is thought that the competitors will benefit more, as the worst scenario is where too few spenders are attracted to an area.

In strict marketing terms we might wish to compare our sales ratios to other sellers/with other types of goods, and we might also choose to analyse our sales per square foot/metre as in large stores but this is probably beyond the scope of this book for what might be for the more amateur practitioners. In reality the professional buyer and seller is more likely to rely on intuition and gut feelings, and in particular the size of the wad of notes as takings for the day.

Negotiating Skills

In this context we are looking at the buying and selling of goods to achieve the best deal for us at the time. It goes without saying that when selling we want the highest possible price for our goods, and when buying we want to pay the lowest possible price for the goods. In the loosest possible terms, negotiating is the offering (usually money) in return for goods (as objects) or "If I ...., You do............," where it can include goods, actions or services.

As a buyer, we may ask how much the seller is seeking for a good, and then negotiate around that price usually at a lower level. It might sometimes save some time and effort by asking the seller at the outset, "what is your very best price (or the death) on this item". If both parties are dealers we may also appeal for the best trade price.

On occasions the seller may ask for a very modest price and we might not see any point in haggling for what is a very fair price. If conversely, the seller is asking for a very high price we may not choose to negotiate at all, and to walk away. This is not a problem if we can easily find the same item elsewhere but if it is a rare item we might not have much choice in the matter, as the owner cannot be forced to part with an item. The law of supply and demand comes in here.

The condition of the goods in question is usually the first thing to influence the price where there is some blemish or damage. The negotiation will then hinge on how little or how much the blemish or damage will affect the price in each opinion. Then other factors that may differentiate the price are age, rarity, quality and make might come into the haggling.

In the hardest of negotiations we might hear the seller who is being squeezed by the price offered reply that "you're trying to take the food from my children's mouths!". This and similar comments may help to get a seller a more reasonable offer by getting the buyer to 'back off'. Other exclamations that I have encountered as a buyer when asking if the goods are in working order, and to counter a claim of possibly faulty goods and consequently a low price, was "On my child's eyes it works, Guv'nor" (This Dickensian response was in the 1970's Cheshire Street Market as it was then by a totter wearing a velvet collared coat and bowler hat who on selling a single item would disappear into "The Carpenters Arms" Public House until all was spent).

A buyer in offering a ridiculously low price for goods may act by testing the resolve of the seller, who might give in easily especially if it is starting to rain or snow. Also, listening to a seller's life history by saying " they don't make them like that any more" may also result in a lower price where it is felt that their treasured goods are being passed on to, and cared for by a friend.

Another ploy for both the buyer and seller after agreeing an outline price is to ask for or offers another item to be "thrown in" to clinch the sale. The additional item could be something that the seller finds it hard to shift, or that the buyer finds could have hidden value (and needs to be researched).

The idea of throwing in another item is particularly useful where the main subject of interest to the buyer is an absurdly and obstinately high price by the seller, e.g. because he paid a higher price than offered and would lose on the deal, or it belonged to his mother and she would turn in her grave if it was sold for that price, but who would almost give away another item of interest with no sentimental value and this would in effect balance out the price.

More recently I have come across a buyer who can shorten negotiations by offering an odd sum of money which is far short of the asking price of £20 but which confounds the seller who would otherwise follow the "let's split the difference" which could now be too much bother to work out so he agrees the price. Meanwhile, the seller is still thinking why the odd 73p? This ploy may not be as daft as it may sound, especially if it applied to larger sums.

When an item is of interest to one or more buyers it may cause some complications or ill-feeling, but it can only be good news for the seller. Most commonly a potential buyer may pick up an item showing their interest and asking the seller the price, and if too high, the goods are put down. This buyer may later return to make a far lower offer to the seller, which might be accepted if little interest has been shown and the sale is about to close.

On occasions a second buyer may be waiting for the first buyer either to buy or put the goods down so that he may jump in and buy them. The first buyer put the goods down without agreeing a price but remained in front of the stall. The second buyer picked up the goods and quickly paid for them. The first buyer might have protested and even fist-cuffs may have followed. As the deal was only completed when the money was paid to the seller the opportunity to haggle over the price in this situation was not possible, and ready cash may have been needed to push into the seller's hand. This is not an ideal situation for either of the buyers and the second buyer must have made up his mind to pay the price quoted to the first buyer, and the first buyer lost his chance to negotiate.

Quiet often we might wish to use the "ugly sisters" approach to buy goods that might otherwise be described as sleepers. Here, we look around the real item of value so as not to alert the seller, and perhaps show interest in lesser goods (the ugly sisters) and we might ask how much to 'throw in' the item of desire as a 'by the way'. The sleeper as can also often appear at auctions when some reason the appearance of the good does not reveal itself to untrained eyes and we hope that this has not been spotted.

Legal Matters

Probably the contractual issues come to mind first of all but we also need to look at some of the legal pitfalls which could cost us dearly. For very small sums of money this may be of little concern to us. But some antiques and collectables may involve hundreds if not thousands of pounds. Matters of provenance will however, be very important for expensive items in proving their value and can form a part of the contract.

As recycling and mainly second hand goods are our main focus in this book, many parts of the Consumer Protection Act and Trades Description Act and other similar Acts may not necessarily apply here as these mainly relate to new goods, manufacturers and often large retail outlets. Guarantees and such-like are not likely apply to old goods and the relevant manufacturers and retailers might no longer exist. Registered antique dealers and auction houses come the nearest to this, but many sales may take place not between dealers, but between private collectors.

From 'time immemorial' public markets within set opening times have historically had some protection under the "Market Overt" rules which meant that if we inadvertently purchased stolen goods that we would not have a legal liability to return them to their rightful owner. However, on the 17 June 1994 a Bill was passed to abolish the market overt law. So beware that even if we buy items in good faith, it is possible that if discovered the original owner would have the right to reclaim the goods regardless of the monies paid.

What is important under contract law is that the representation of the goods that induced the buyer to hand over cash to the seller, was true as far as the seller knew and that false information would be described as a misrepresentation and he/she could be sued for in the civil courts. Again, in a market place, flea market or car boot sale for example receipts are not common, let alone the name of the seller, or the fact that he or she may not be a regular seller at that location so such redress in most circumstances is not a likely proposition. We must therefore accept a limited risk in the money that we are prepared to spend in such situations. Up to £50 may be reasonable to some people.

The sale of a good and the contract itself may result from a series of offers and counter-offers. Each new offer cancels the previous offer. When a price has finally been agreed along with any representations (such as age, condition, quality, & maker) that induce the sale by the seller, the money is then handed over in return for the goods (consideration).

A refund of monies paid is not necessarily an option following the contract which is formed. It might only be if we are disappointed with the goods that we find are broken after buying them that a reasonable seller might offer a refund, but he/she does not have to. To force the issue of a refund we need to be looking at a breach of contract or misrepresentation and take this to the small claims court for claims up to the value of £5,000. Local Trading Standards offices may keep a list of complaints made against regular traders but to some extent with second hand goods it is a case of caveat emptor (buyer beware).

Although the contract may be unwritten as such the procedure followed creates the contract. If the sale price monies or the goods were not transferred, then no contract exists. It would only be if the goods sold did not match the seller's description or any relevant representation made that a breach of contract might exist and can be sued for in the civil courts.

If a seller knew nothing about his goods for sale, or made up some fantastic representation about them we should use our own discretion by looking before buying. In fact sometimes it is to our advantage to buy from ignorant sellers as the price of the goods can only be truly assessed and classified with all of the information. So if we buy goods at face value and later research shows that we have a valuable and rare item it is to our advantage, although equally we could make a loss. We need to research the type of goods that we are looking for and the likely values.

If we are no longer talking about spending the odd £50 and are to spend a lot more we must ask for a receipt from the seller (even in a private sale) that preferably gives a detailed description of the goods sold, and this confirms the contract made. As with the purchase of more expensive goods we can gain more protection by buying from established dealers but in turn we will pay more and are unlikely to get a bargain as such.

As a point of interest, it is only the sale of real estate that requires a detailed written contract which is to be exchanged. Many other contracts tend to relate to employment, the large scale sale and supply of goods, and most commonly to the supply of services, but also building contracts which include a detailed specification of works.

Ethical matters might include for example, the purchase or selling of ivory, the skins, the shells, of rare species of animals and possibly any items that might be considered as offensive such as elephant foot dustbins and/or in bad taste and there may be an undercover market in this area which is beyond the scope of this book.

However, for antique ivory goods we are allowed to trade in those that have been manufactured prior to 1 June 1947 so some provenance might help but the style and aging will also help to decide this. The UK and EU Law applies here in conjunction with CITES (Convention International Trade in Endangered Species).

The sale of some turtles and tortoise shell items may be allowed but similarly restricted to non-endangered species. Also the sale of stuffed birds may be restricted to captive-bred waterfowl and game birds. Migratory specimens are not allowed.

Electrical appliances, especially if old can be in a hazardous condition in terms of the electrocution of the user, or being the cause of a fire. Whilst most people are capable of fitting a plug or changing a fuse, they may not be able to decide the correct fuse rating of an appliance, to check that the appliance is correctly earthed or to replace a cable that has perished and crumbling insulation. It is hoped that readers are more than capable of doing so under supervision, but if you are not sure get it checked out by a qualified and experienced electrician. If an unchecked electrical item is sold by auctioneers they may insist that the plug and lead is cut off.

When second-hand, or re-upholstered furniture (foam and non-foam) made after 1 January 1950 is sold it is required to meet the fire resistance standards of the Furniture and Furnishings (Fire) (Safety) Regulations 1988 (amended 1989 and 1883). In new and re-upholstered furniture following the introduction of these regulations a display label is required to be fitted to indicate that the fire resistance standards have been met. If we should chose to sell post 1 January 1950's furniture at auction that does not meet this standard they are not likely to be accepted into their salesroom.

Where the history of an item has prime importance to its value it is essential to have written or photographic evidence and details of the previous ownership and where it came from to back this up claim which is normally referred to as the 'provenance'. Where this provenance is not available the price must be adjusted accordingly or we may well decide not to purchase the goods at all.

Sometimes the most elaborate stories relating to an item such as medals and militaria by war-time comrades may be used to back-up the provenance. When it comes to celebrity signatures it may be necessary to research other documents signed by the star to see if they match.

Without the provenance the value of, for example an unsigned sculpture, figure, bust, etching, watercolour or oil on canvas (and other forms of art) the value can vary greatly and may depend on an expert's decision. Without expert advice we may risk paying much more than we should for such works of art. However, at an auction or with a dealer we might hope to find a degree of honesty and we may need to rely on descriptions. An example might be "in the manner of", or "in the style of" 'Thurkettle' of the Norwich School of Watercolourists". So in such cases where we cannot directly attribute a piece of art to a particular artist, the price should be far more modest than perhaps an original.

Unlike precious metals like gold and silver which are normally hallmarked, along with high quality ceramics which also have markings to help identify them, some antiques and other works of art do not. Apart from the attribution of a work of art the materials it is made of can have a great deal of effect on the value of the item in question.

Examples include a resin bust in relation to a marble bust, or a spelter sculpture in relation to a bronze sculpture. In both cases the former is worth a lot less than the latter. For example in the latter, the finish and/or the patination can be very deceptive along with the weight.

A spelter figure with a plaster filled base to add weight would be hard to tell from a bronze. So the buyer must beware. With the matter of materials used and the attribution there is much scope for deception. As we are unlikely to have an expert to hand when we are searching for a bargain we must rely on our own research and experience. The handling of these goods is all important to learning about such areas of specialism.

On a lighter note there may be many more legal and illegal issues to be considered which are beyond the scope of this book. However, readers of Jonathan Gash and viewers of television's 'Lovejoy' may be familiar with some enjoyable "flights of fantasy" that might contain some essence of reality with illegal activities such as 'rings' (Cartels of dealers) at auctions who may artificially keep prices low or sometimes high and later share in the proceeds, are one of the many scams to be seen.

In Lovejoy 'copyists' appear to be highly valued craftsmen and only if they are prosecuted are they known as forgers, and of course the swapping of the genuine articles with fakes is common practice.

The 'distressing' of newly made "antiques" is carried out by hitting the object with chains and acid etching to give the appearance old age and antiquity as the design would lead a potential buyer to believe.

We might wish to make up our own minds on what was the truth or fiction with this television series. It is recommended as highly watchable although not always believable or realistic, although the glamour of antiques is balanced with 'going on the knock' (collecting from door to door) and 'bin diving' for antiques.

EXAMPLES

Antiques and Collectibles – Misc.

Art Nouveau Style Bust

I purchased this bust at a car boot sale for about £3 and it was supplied in a cardboard box containing the base and most of the shoulders with the head and part of the shoulder in four pieces. It had obviously been broken and the owner was keen that someone would take it off of their hands. I liked the Art Nouveau style and it appeared to have been from the Edwardian period. I was very concerned that this should not end up in the rubbish tip.

The starting point was to have a clear table with all parts being carefully laid out. Even lose chips and fragments were examined for future use. It was now possible to deal with this project as being like a jigsaw puzzle and to search for the location of each part.

It was possible to deal with the assembly of these parts in different orders. I chose to treat the base with shoulders as one part to which I would add the assembled four parts of the head and part shoulder. I did however find that any errors in the alignment of the smaller parts could add up to a greater mismatch when offered up to the main base of the bust and some filling would be required.

The material of the bust was Plaster of Paris and a suitable glue for porous materials like this was essential. Some masking tape was helpful in holding individual parts together whilst the glue set. The finished assembly now indicated where parts would need to be rubbed down to blend in, and smoothed out ready to be touched in with paint.

I was able to identify various colours that could be found in the 'Humbrol' range, in particular being the flesh colour as a matt finish paint. These paints are commonly found in modellers' shops for use with airfix models and the like. Where colours could not be matched oil paints could be blended to suit and a clear varnish used to obtain a gloss finish.

I was pleased with the finished result but I found it hard to locate the bust in a suitable place within my house. The striking colours made it hard to match with other household décor. Also the value of the bust is not likely to be high being made of plaster but I was pleased with an auction house estimate of about £45. So fortunately this item will be recycled not to the dustbin, but to a new owner who will be aware of the restoration.

Ballot Box

The ballot box with some damage and loose beading was purchased for £3 at a car boot sale. The box relates to applicants for membership to exclusive clubs and societies where the members or committee can ballot to accept or reject a candidate.

A box containing small white balls was found within the ballot box. Also the name of Toye & Co Ltd at the back of the box may be Toye, Kenning & Spencer well known for its Royal, Military and Masonic (and other) regalia.

I believe that each voter was issued with a (white) ball which they could put secretly through the front of the ballot box, into either the left or right of the two small drawers bellow. Each these two drawers corresponds with the a letter 'Y' for yes for acceptance and the letter 'N' for no for rejection. I think that the expression of being "black balled" for a rejection which may have come from this process. But regardless of this being the case, it is an interesting item.

It was necessary to strip the box of the 'Y' and 'N' letters, the beading, the rim of the opening and the two drawers. The cracks then needed to be filled and the whole box sanded down, the beading refitted and then varnished. The letters were then refitted and the drawers and the base were relined with blue velvet.

The box now looking like its original condition makes an interesting conversation piece, and I believe that it might fetch perhaps between £30 to £50 at auction should I become tired of it or need more space.

Coffee Pot – Mason's

This coffee pot caught my eye in a charity shop at what I thought to be a fair price of £4.95p. The condition was as new and a make of Mason's was shown underneath, with the pattern of 'Mandalay' also being shown. The bold colours which include a cobalt blue made it particularly attractive. It clearly belonged, and would be more valuable as a part of a larger set of this pattern, rather than being used by me as a coffee pot on its own. It was now clear to me that it needed to be recycled and luckily for me on this occasion that no restoration was required.

I decided to look up the details of this coffee pot and found a similar example on e-bay for £35. It became clear that there was a demand for the Mandalay pattern for those who had missing items from a full service, possibly because of breakages. My occasional usage of this item as a coffee pot on its own, was now outweighed by the demand for missing items to a complete collection of this pattern.

Having not known the possible value of this item on purchase I was pleased with my decision to buy, but I now felt that as it was potentially of more value as a missing part of a set, so that I preferred to sell this coffee pot.

This is one example where no work (or missing parts) was required in order to sell at a profit. Apart from advertising on e-bay and finding a suitable sized box along with wrapping I was able sell this item for £39. Although I do not consider myself to be a dealer, this was one rare example of being able to recover some of the expenses incurred from other projects.

Incidentally, as a regular donor to this charity shop with many of my (no longer required) recycled goods being sold at this charity shop, I do not feel that I have gained any special advantage with this purchase, especially as I was not previously aware of the true value of the coffee pot.

Food Cover

This food cover was found to be over 100 years old and possibly Victorian. It was bought from a car boot sale for £3 as the handle had broken off and it was in a filthy condition shown as above. Food covers were often used to cover a plate or a bowl of hot food on a tray to keep it warm as it was taken from the kitchen to the dining room. They do sometimes have a matching tray of the same size but, even without a tray and broken handle this was still a bargain.

The food cover was thoroughly cleaned using a non-abrasive scouring pad and silver polish giving a reasonably good finish although some wear and tear was shown with some minor dents and scratches when examined closely. I was then able to see the markings inside the silver plated cover which indicated the maker being Fenton Bros. (est. in 1859) and an indication of the year of manufacture as 1863 making this item about 150 years old.

I now looked at the handle and it was clear that the original fixing screw was missing and the thread which was probably a ¼" British Standard Whitworth in the handle had been stripped leaving about a ¼" diameter hole. I decided to use the next thread size up being a 5/16" Whitworth to drill and tap a new thread. Using a suitable size of screw this allowed the handle to be re-fitted. I did notice that the handle made of a soft material similar to pewter did not initially fit closely to the shape of the cover dome and was probably damaged when the handle came off. It required some shaping with a soft mallet and filing to the underside to give it a close fit as was originally intended. See the finished picture below.

The missing matching metal tray for this food cover (if there ever was one) would have been ideal to complete this project although it is usable on its own, and I have put this on my 'wish list' as something to look out for in the future (I carry a folded paper template of the cover base for this purpose). However, I have found that this food cover can be matched with any normal oval dinner sized plate, sometimes used for steak dinners.

These food covers can sometimes be in demand for banquets and or even kept for the Christmas Turkey dinner to make it more of a special treat. Although I cannot find any good examples of similar items for sale except for the more precious ones in solid silver at several hundred pounds. This must be worth at least £20 which is far more than the £3 paid in poor condition.

Thimble – Acorn Case

This is an example of what can be made on a small lathe. The materials that can be used include Tagua Nut, Sycamore, Boxwood and other hardwoods may be used after seasoning. A fine grain structure is preferable especially if the thimble holder and its lid are to screw together and a fine finish is possible.

It should be possible to salvage a variety of hardwoods from possible broken furniture, unfinished projects and/or unfashionable wooden goods that may no longer be saleable and can be reused. Apart from the usual car boot sales, salvage yards may also be of use. As seasoning takes place over a period of years the use of older recycled timber is to our advantage.

Antique thimble holders can be fairly expensive and so a reproduction case if well-made can be worth about £25 as a minimum, with good examples fetching more than £100. So if you wished to have a profitable hobby then this could for you.

Collectors include those who like sewing memorabilia, and treen will be interested along with those of a general interest who just like fine detailed boxes which is what caught my interest in the first place.

Designs can vary and using both light and dark coloured woods with say a dark lid and light holder can be very attractive. Instead of threaded cases a push on lid can be used which is easier to produce. Whilst the general shape of a thimble case may be like an acorn another design such as that of a skep is also a good shape. Whilst the picture above shows a diamond pattern on the lid I believe that annular grooves around the curvature of the lid are also attractive. At either end of the thimble case finials of much more detail than that shown above may be used, and tassels on the finials add to the design if required.

Another variation which may require an enlargement or elongation of the case is that of housing a small sewing kit including the thimble. These sewing kit holders do exist and some research may be necessary to decide how it should be laid out. Alternatively, we can decide what should be included in such a kit such as needles, thread and the thimble and then how it will be accommodated.

We might also need to know how thimble sizes may vary including precious ones which may need housing. A precious thimble for example made of gold and having turquoise stones positioned around it might need us to customise a case to suit. However, although many silver thimbles exist which may be someone's pride and joy we need an idea of perhaps the largest, smallest and the average thimble size.

DRINK RELATED

Barrels – Oak

This smaller of the two barrels (about one gallon) was purchased at a car boot sale for £7. I would hope to use this for a particular type of cider such as still or sparkling, or even Perry from pears, while using the larger barrel shown over page (about 5 gallons) for ordinary cider.

Both of the barrels suffered from similar problems which needed to be addressed before they could be used again as barrels. The main problem being that over many years without use and being empty and dry the wooden staves had shrunk which would cause the barrel to leak.

Firstly, in each case the barrels needed to be exposed to water which over a period of time would allow the staves to expand to create a water tight vessel. (I think that the larger of the two barrels which had been converted into a padded seat may have actually been positioned next to a fire which may have contributed to it drying out).

Secondly, having allowed the exposure of the staves to water over a period of time, and if there is still a severe leakage of water, the hoops around the barrel may need to be re-positioned. Nails securing the hoops must be first removed. In particular, the two hoops either side of the bulge in the middle of the barrel can be individually moved closer to centre forcing the staves closer together. The top and bottom hoops may also be adjusted if necessary, but will have less effect.

Thirdly, the barrel now needs to be tested again for water tightness. At this stage it should be possible to fill the barrel to the top, and to assess how much is leaking, bearing in mind that it is only at this stage the staves can be fully soaked for any period of time, and that now their final expansion will seal the barrel as leakage becomes progressively smaller.

The barrel shown immediately above was purchased from a car boot sale for £20 with the top end originally covered with padding and a fabric covering for use as a seat. It can be seen in the above photo where the seat materials had been stapled to the top.

After I had stripped off the seat it became clear that the barrel was formerly used by Bulmers of Hereford for cider and I would hope to also use it for the same purpose in conjunction with the fruit press also shown in this book. I later established that the barrel has a capacity of about 5 gallons and this was ideal for my purposes.

The restored oak barrel (below) I believe will complement the traditional making of cider that I am hoping to make in the coming years.

These barrels made of real oak wood by the traditional skills of a Cooper are something that I treasure along with many other crafts.

The cleaning of the barrel where necessary before use requires some additional consideration, as well as some form of sterilisation. Any odd smells or debris flushed out might confirm that the barrel needs cleaning and sterilising, and it would be better prevent the waste of a brew and the possibility of illness from drinking it (See Pooley & Lomax "Real Cider Making").

Pebbles or brass chain shaken in the barrel may dislodge any further debris which can then be flushed out. The next step is to fill the barrel with washing soda at a ratio of 125g per gallon and left for two days with occasional turning/agitation. The soda in the barrel then needs to be neutralised using a solution of 30g of Citric Acid per gallon, followed by regular flushing with clean water. Then drain and bung up for a week.

The sterilization is carried out by using a solution of 6 Campden tablets with 10g of Citric Acid per pint of water. The resulting fumes should be avoided as a potential hazard. The solution should then be kept and agitated in the bunged barrel, until use, when it should be flushed with much cold water leaving it ready for use.

Barrel – Large, Stand

This 'would be' director's chair was purchased for £3 at a car boot sale.

If we can visualise the arms and backrest removed and 2 straps or padding at the two front and the 2 rear places instead of the canvas seat cover, the 5 gallon barrel will be slung or propped horizontally with the tap accessible from the front (See photo below).

The removal of the arms was simple, by undoing the hinges each side of the seat. The canvas backrest needed to be cut off where it doubled around the back supports.

The canvas seat itself was held into a groove either side of the base. When the seat is removed it will need to be replaced with two straps spread apart at the front and rear of the base, or padding at the four corners to account for the support to the narrower ends of the barrel.

As shown below with the barrel in position the padding can be arranged to allow the tap end to be lower to assist with the draining of the contents and to continue the supply of drink as the quantity reduces. This is ideal perhaps, for street parties and barbeques. The barrel as positioned on the stand is shown in the photo below. A small bucket can be hung from the tap to catch any drips from the pouring of the drinks.

The hinged stays that fix the amount that the 'X' frame can open have been repositioned to reduce the width of the frame in use, and this conveniently raises the height of the barrel slightly for easier access to the tap without stooping too much. The stand itself when folded will close down to 3" wide making it easy to store.

Decanting Machine

This was purchased at an antiques market for £25. It appears to be a reproduction of an old design especially having a candle holder to show that the sediment within the bottle from vintage port or claret for example, is kept within the bottle rather than passed out through the neck of the bottle into the decanter. These decanting machines are often owned by wine connoisseurs who may have a cellar full of bottles of fine vintage wine and normally retail for over £200.

The winding mechanism designed to tilt the bottle gradually downwards was sticking and the also needed some adjustment on the linkages to the cradle. I made a number of adjustments and oiled the screw and linkages so that it worked smoothly.

Although I only have one or two old bottles of port, I very much enjoyed owning and playing with this "toy". I have since purchased a simpler but better quality decanting machine from a car boot sale for £12 as most people did not know what it was for, and I chose to put the one shown in for auction and it fetched £55.

This is one of a number of items in this book that I could not have justified or dreamt of owning at £200+ yet they have given me a lot of pleasure.

Fruit Press

The fruit press is shown in its restored condition. It was bought at a car boot sale for £8 with some parts missing. In particular the central screw shown in front of the press was fitted but importantly without a nut to carry out the pressing function.

The screw thread on the central screw that was fitted was of an unusual type and it was not possible get a nut that would fit.

Finally a visit to the suppliers of a similar type of fruit press retailing for about £120, each was examined only to find that this type of thread was no longer used and a replacement nut would not be the solution. But I did establish that the diameter and pitch of the old screw supplied could be replaced with that a smaller diameter and finer pitched thread that could be a 16mm threaded stud of the same length and welded to the underside of the base of the press. This area was made bare ready for welding.

The new threaded stud was cut to the required overall length and secured within the existing hole in the base with a nut on either side. The nut above the base would be removed after welding, whilst the nut below the base would be welded on each of its sides to the base with the stud being welded within the threaded area of the nut. On cooling, the top nut was removed leaving the stud supported rigidly and at right angles and central to the base.

At this point with some damage to the existing paintwork on the base from the welding and the new bare metal in the weld area it was necessary to prepare and repaint the whole of the base. Also the hoops and staves that contain the fruit while pressing needed to be taken apart for cleaning and the repainting of the hoops.

The whole press was reassembled ready for use. It looked like new and for a total cost of about £15 it was a huge saving on the new cost of about £120. I am now ready to make apple or pear drinks from windfall fruits.

Fruit Press – Ratchet Lever

Some fruit presses I believe came with a bulky 'capstan' threaded system on the central screw nut where the tommy bar could be inserted in three positions in each rotation, to make the pressing easier. As technology gathers pace, the socket wrenches for mechanics (not suitable for our use) have long been available and they now include "open ended" ring spanners having built in ratchets that allow the central screw to pass through the centre as shown above.

This is ideal for our use on the fruit press especially in place of the spanner shown in the earlier restoration above where the tightening process of squeezing the crushed fruit involved turning the ring spanner end perhaps a quarter of a turn at a time, then removing it from the nut and then re-engaging the nut to turn it again, and so on. The new spanner with ratchet will only require say a quarter of a turn or less before reversing it, to again reapply pressure without having to disengage the spanner from the nut each time.

The photo below shows the ratchet end of the spanner.

Tantalus

Although I already had a nice pair of Crystal cut glass decanters I had always wanted a 'tantalus' as a complete lockable unit.

I later found in a charity shop for the sum of £8 – the missing part to go with my existing decanters to make a 'tantalus'. This consisted of an oak and brass framework with a handle at the top, and a hinged lockable bottom front which allowed the decanters to be slid in and out, and locked when not in use. Hence the name – to tantalise, the would be drinker, possibly a servant or member of staff. The design was a reproduction of a traditional design probably no more than about 30 years of age but of good quality. The original decanters were probably broken or used separately, and the key question at the time of purchase was whether or not my own decanters would fit.

As in many cases a decision to buy was made without, in this case, the decanters that would be required to fit. I later found that they did fit, but too tightly. It would be necessary to tackle two areas to solve this problem, one being the top of the decanter stoppers, and the other being the underside of the top rail of the tantalus.

This adjustment was easily made and the tantalus was ready for use.

FURNITURE

Chair – Corner

This Edwardian corner chair was a gift from a friend for my unpaid help with clearing a deceased relative's house, but the treatment of woodworm was not straightforward. The chemical treatment for about £5 injected into the wormholes brought activity to a halt. But as the seat was to be re-upholstered the webs and cover would not be likely to hold in a honeycomb of worm holes. The strength of this frail Edwardian chair was questioned as it might be unsafe to use.

It became necessary to inject a resin to fill the worm holes which would consolidate the wooden structure of the chair making it strong and usable again. Once this had dried out the frame was sanded down, stained and varnished. I decided to match the original shade and finish of the chair as in the photo.

It was now ready for upholstery. The first step was to tack on the webs, woven from back to front and side to side of the chair seat making each web sufficiently taut. The filling included horse hair with a layer of wadding. This wadding was capped with a layer of calico to compress the stuffing evenly ready for the cover. The red velvet fabric was cut to fit over the seat accounting for the "lay" of the velvet and pulled tight for tacking in place. To finish, I decided fit gilt braid with gimp pins to cover the edge of the velvet. Also a black dust cover was fitted under the seat to finish off.

The additional cost of the resin treatment was about £20 before the actual restoration had started. Overall, the cost of the finishing and upholstery came to about another £30 and had I paid for the chair I would not have recovered its value following the total cost of restoration. However, I was pleased with the finished chair and it has earned a useful place in my house.

Chair – Prie Dieu (Prayer)

This prayer chair was purchased for £7 at a car boot sale. I knew it was "special" in its design and that it was used by kneeling on the seat and supporting one's elbows on the top of the backrest with hands clasped together in prayer. In the backrest of the chair is a carved form of a cross. The rush seat was in good condition. The chair itself was rigid and I recognised that the high back of the chair fitted to a low seat had a weak spot where it joins the base of the chair seat, especially with the top of the back as a resting point.

The main fault was that of signs of woodworm across the whole of the dark brown finished wooden chair frame. I stored the chair in a large sealed refuse sack until I was ready to work on it to avoid any spread to other wooden items.

I later found little or no evidence of wood dust within the bag showing active woodworm but I decided to carry out woodworm treatment to be sure that there was no trace. I took the chair into the garden and using a brush I covered the whole of the wooden frame with woodworm chemicals paying extra attention to areas with many flight holes. The frame was then left out to dry to let the chemical smells disappear. Fortunately, the woodworm holes had not noticeably reduced the strength of the chair although I consider it to be of decorative rather than for practical usage. Certainly there was no crumbling of the wooden frame in places as is common in the worst examples of worm damage.

To finish off the chair as shown in the picture above, a wide paint brush was used to brush on a dark brown wax polish ensuring that the wax entered and covered any wood worm holes that were visible. When the wax polish had dried this process was repeated several times until a smooth and durable finish was achieved.

This chair which was now useable was also very attractive and decorative. With the chair positioned in front of a light coloured wall the shape of the chair to be clearly seen to its best advantage.

Dinner Gong

The gong itself was purchased for £10 without the frame to hang it from. It took some time to decide how and when I would be able to use it. It was a project that was waiting to be progressed until I stumbled across what was a fire screen in a charity shop. Initially I considered the barley twists alone as materials for a frame for the gong, and I purchased the screen for £5.

When I got home and positioned the gong in front screen I could see that the size and the style (possibly 1940's) were right as a frame for the gong. All that was required was the removal of a tapestry covered panel in the middle of the screen to see an outline of the finished article.

The tapestry and an inner frame were carefully removed with no damage except for some small holes for the dowel fixings. These were later filled in and the finishes were made good.

I was very pleased for a period of time that I could be called in for my dinner when hearing the gong in my garden. But later I needed to downsize and this item unfortunately went to auction and fetched £45.

Display Table

This newish item, possibly a reproduction of an older design, was sold as seen from a charity shop for £10 and I would have estimated a new price of about £100 if it were not broken. The glazed panels with bevelled edges were an attractive feature along with the legs/feet which feature often on library furniture. It was noticeable that the glazed lid was not properly fixed in position. By lifting the lid slightly I could see that one hinge had come adrift and was still fixed to a part of the wooden frame which had itself broken away.

This would be difficult to repair and apart from gluing the broken wooden frame it would be likely to remain a weak spot. The frame would need to be reinforced in a very small cross-sectional area of timber and this would not be easy to without it being visible and spoiling the good looks of this attractive piece of furniture.

So, in addition to some careful use of wood glue and clamping of the broken frame in place for several hours, I was able drill and pin the area. The steel pins used were positioned at various angles so that it would not be possible for this part of the frame to break away again in the same spot as before. Taking into account the stresses that act on the hinges such as when the lid is accidentally allowed to fall backwards against the hinges, the hidden pins and a stay (which was not fitted) were successfully able to do the job.

As the pins (after drilling), were driven in with a suitable sized pin punch so that they were placed just below the wooden surface allowing a matching wood filler to hide the pins. The surrounding area of wood was now to be touched in to cover any sign of the repair.

Overall, I am pleased with this restoration which now resembles the original condition when it was first made. The only problem with the design is that it does not offer a very efficient use of floor space in terms of the area that can be displayed as opposed to a vertical display cabinet which may have a number of shelves.

Footstool

This footstool was purchased for £6 at a car boot sale. I particularly wanted this stool to match a black leather buttoned settee, a wing chair and two armchairs. It required some work to be carried out on it in general.

In particular it was in need of scratches to be touched in and the general polishing of the base. The matching of the colour of the red buttoned leather with my existing black leather furniture was going to be a problem. It was necessary to stain the red leather to the colour black. Should the staining of the red leather not be successful, the red hide removed and laid flat could act as a pattern for a replacement cover in black hide, as and when I could get hold of some.

The red hide was carefully brushed over with "permanent black ink" taking care to get into the diamond pleats in the leather and any visible areas. It would need sufficient time to fully dry out. Following the staining which incidentally may be carried out to lighter colours to make them darker, but not the other way round, I examined the cover to find any traces of the original red colour including various shades what might be considered to be a dark red. A second coating of black stain was required to remove any traces of the red.

Having fully dried, with a satisfactory colour finish on the leather footrest top, a good coating of black shoe polish was applied to create a good hard wearing black shine.

The base was then given a thorough coating of a dark wood polish and then shined. The slight scratches and scuffs on the wooden base have now become less noticeable and are fully compatible with what might be a 20 or 30 year old stool that is now ready for another 20 or 30 years of service.

Plant Stand

This reproduction plant stand shown above was purchased at the Newark antiques fair in an unfinished state for £8. It was a part of a job lot of about 2 dozen unfinished stands that were being sold with some of the stands being faulty.

It was necessary to examine before buying to ensure that the legs were not warped, that all parts had been machined correctly, and whether the stand could be stood without rocking. It was clear that none of these stands had been finished with stain and varnish but this would not be difficult to complete.

Firstly, the stand needed to be finished with a fine grade of sandpaper and wire wool. Secondly, having removed any dust the stand was stained to give a dark wood finish. Thirdly, when dry the stand was covered in varnish to give a highly polished finish. This finished reproduction stand would normally cost £50 or more to buy and I feel that I have gained a bargain.

The plant stand was ready for an attractive potted plant, possibly with trailing leaves and flowers.

AUDIO EQUIPMENT – VINTAGE

Horn Loudspeaker

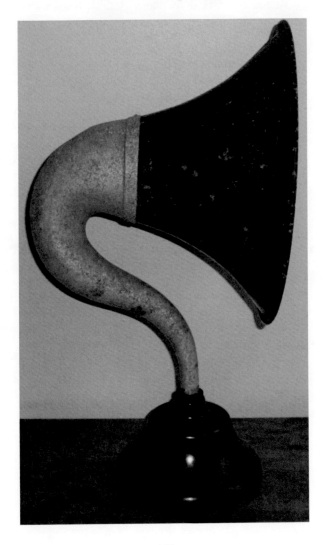

This item was purchased for £10 from a flea-market at Battlesbridge in Essex. The horn appeared to be made of Aluminium with a Bakelite base and in fair condition for its age except for the electrical parts in the base which were missing. This put this speaker at risk of being disposed of, especially if it became dented or cracked in transit. I think that this type of speaker was used in the transition from headphones (as used with crystal sets) to the early valve radios that followed with low outputs and the horn acting as an amplifier to the sound.

The missing parts were not too much of a problem as I did not have a wireless to connect it to, or be likely to own one, but the antiquated design of the early 20th century did give me a buzz as it was truly quirky in comparison with today's equipment. I believe that I was justified in buying this horn loudspeaker as it appealed to me and I would adapt it with minimal changes in the design for another purpose. Only a new baseboard in the horn base will be altered, so the horn could later be restored to its original purpose as a potentially rare and collectable item.

As a concept I decided that if I could fit some very small speakers of the type used with small portable radios and iPods in particular, into the base. In fact a very small amplifier could also be accommodated if necessary. Of course this design would not give the best of stereophonic sound but it would be better than the original mono reproduction. Only a small lead with a jack plug need be visible to link with an early 21st century invention such as the iPod. In fact the two technologies a century apart with perhaps an iPod dock would be even more quirky than having each item on its own.

The restored "concept" Horn Loudspeaker is shown with an
iPod in its dock juxtaposed together, above.

Large Gramophone

The gramophone as shown above is of good quality and is a Columbia "Grafanola" model which has a built in speaker horn and the volume being partly controlled by opening and shutting the louvered front panel (like a Rolls Royce radiator grill of the same period).

I purchased this gramophone at an antiques market for £45 as being in need of repair. The broken item was a gimballed support tube (shown in the photo below as a broken "V" notch joining a hole) for the sound box and the pick up arm where it attached the gramophone base and loudspeaker horn. One of the pivot points of the gimballed support tube had broken away where the hole for the pivot screw fitted and I needed to make a new support tube.

As I had recently acquired a Unimat 4 lathe I knew that this was an ideal turning job that I could tackle as a repair project. The replacement support tube can be seen in the photo of the lathe at the bottom where I had just bored out what would become the gimballed section of the support tube where two pivot screws will be fitted after drilling and tapping. Here, I have used mild steel as a stronger material than the type of alloy used originally, to prevent the same breakage from occurring.

The only problem here is that of rust on the finished item which will be partly visible when the gramophone lid is open. Here I have decided that a polished and lacquered finish will be adequate in this case, along with oil on the moving parts. I hope in the future to set up a nickel plating vat for small items such as the support tube, but unless there is a number of items to plate at the same time the space taken cannot always be justified. Otherwise, a number of items from several projects (which may in each case be held up) need to be scheduled for the same time.

Now that the new support tube has been fitted, as seen in the photo above (the broken part is positioned alongside of it) the gramophone is now complete and in good working order. In theory the gramophone should now be worth its full value for this model which should be at about twice the purchase price. However, I shall enjoy the nostalgia of playing my old 78's on it.

The Portable Gramophone

This Columbia Grafonola (the same make and model as above but as a portable version) gramophone cost me £8 at a car boot sale and although the sound box which holds the gramophone needle was missing, the main body of the machine was in better than usual condition. Also, I had a spare sound box from another gramophone.

The exterior of the gramophone had a blue 'Rexine' finish which appeared little worn. In addition to this, were travel labels as normally found on old suit cases, from world travels including the 'White Star' cruise line, had to some extent protected it from damage. However, the labels were in poor condition and had to be removed leaving an 'as new' condition in places. The blue finish after cleaning all over was touched in on some minor spots of wear using navy blue touch up paint for shoes.

The carrying handle had its leather 'covering' strap missing showing only the inner spring steel part of the handle. I was able to buy a similar new strap handle from which the missing leather covering was removed, trimmed to length, and painted navy blue with the above touch up paint and fitted to the existing handle. Also the rubber feet were missing from the underside of the case and similar rubber plugs were made from 'Supatap' sink washers to fit in the holes left from the previous feet (now unobtainable).

Having found the replacement sound box from a similar scrapped portable gramophone I was able to fit this in place of the missing one. The playing mechanism was wound up and I was now able to play an old 78 rpm record that I had available. The gramophone played well and looked surprisingly good for its age. The value should I wish to sell the gramophone would be well in excess of the money paid for it. But I may in the future take this portable gramophone out on a picnic or when boating on a river.

Loud Hailer

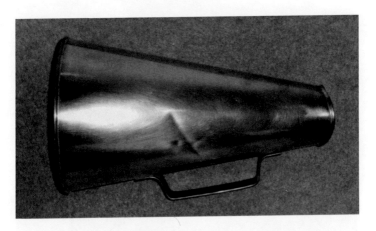

This item was purchased for £8 in an antiques market and I believe that it is quirky with its novelty value and that it could be used by boating enthusiasts to communicate to the crew in strong winds.

The only work carried out on this was to bring the shape back to being a circular cone from what was oval, and then to polish the exterior. Although it is not advisable to remove the original patina of such brass items, but in this case the finish was poor and did require a reasonable surface finish. It can be seen that there are some dents which I would not attempt to remove as these help to confirm the age and history of this item.

One can only guess at the history of this loud hailer from perhaps the training at a distance for athletes such as runners, cyclists or rowers, to the general commercial dock work of instructing the loading and unloading cargo, to leisure sailors from the Skipper guiding the crew in setting the sails and rigging.

LAMPS

Armillary Sphere Lamp

This lamp was purchased for £4 at a car boot sale. The design of the armillary sphere was quite popular at the time, especially in sun dials but it was as a lamp that I believe made it both useful and attractive. Being made of brass also gave it an old and scientific appearance. Unfortunately, as with many such bargains as this, we can expect either some damage and/or missing parts. In this case the arrow through the sphere was missing the arrowhead at one end.

As a replacement (brass) arrowhead was not going to be easy to find I had to consider my options. The arrowhead would not resemble an actual arrowhead in being sharp and pointed, but it would need to be blunt and not too pointed for safety reasons. A possible replacement that came to mind was that of the ends fitted to curtain support poles, although many other designs were made. I was not able to find such a fitting and I believed that if I had it might have been made of plastic with a gold finish and not a good substitute.

The rod through the sphere was threaded at each end with 5/16" British Standard Fine thread, and so the width of any material used would need to be of at least 3/8" of an inch in thickness at that point. So to fabricate an arrowhead we would need some brass plate of perhaps 3/16" thick cut to the arrow shape with a piece of 3/8" diameter round brass bar (drilled and tapped 5/16" BSF at one end) to be brazed to the back end of the arrowhead. All of the edges were then be rounded off and then all of it polished and finished with a clear lacquer. Although it is pointed the width of the point makes it blunt, from a safety aspect.

The arrowhead now fitted to the sphere looked original and the completed lamp looked a bargain. This is now both a functional and decorative item.

It is strongly advised that only a qualified or trained person should carry the rewiring of household items, and where this is not possible, the inspection of the finished item by an electrician is recommended, particularly where the finished goods have exposed metal surfaces.

Lamp – Bouillotte Style

This tin shaded three candle electric lamp was quite a find but had it been larger it would have made an ideal desk lamp that I am unfortunately still looking for. The lamp cost me £4 at a car boot sale and it was rather dirty and neglected. The 3 bulbs fitted were of an unusual size in terms of fixing and voltage and lead me to believe the lamp was of a foreign origin. This raised the question of whether I would be able to use the lamp here in the UK. In fact the lamp is in the French style I believe to be known as bouillotte with 3 tolle (candle) lamp.

The bulbs were secured by what I would describe as a medium Edison screw fixing and the voltage was 110 volts. If I was not able to find matching 240 volt bulbs with the same size of Edison screw fixing the lamp might not be usable. The use of 240 volts in this lamp instead of 110 volts would not be a technical or health & safety problem as it is the loading (in Amps) which is more crucial and it is intended only to use low wattage bulbs.

Having been to a number of suppliers of lamp bulbs it was a specialist shop that was able to match the unusual Edison screw thread size (not the normal medium or similar size) and with a voltage of 240 volts, but unfortunately of a very low output of 7 watts. These bulbs were the only size stocked and they were meant for the use in nightlights. However, 3 times 7 watts meant a total of 21 watts and this made the lamp usable, perhaps on a hall table.

The electrical side of the this lamp especially because its mainly metal construction, meant that it should be earthed to a high standard as any short circuit could potentially electrocute someone touching any part of the lamp. I decided to rewire the lamp with new 3 core flex with a gold finish to match the gold lined paintwork with a 2 amp fuse rating at the plug. The lamp was now safe to use.

The finish on the lamp required some careful polishing and it now looked an attractive and useful lamp.

It is strongly advised that only a qualified or trained person should carry out the rewiring of household items, and where this is not possible, the inspection of the finished item by an electrician is recommended, particularly where the finished goods have exposed metal surfaces.

Lamps – Brass Oil

I purchased the two matching lamps on separate occasions at car boot sales for around about £6 to £8 each without the glass chimneys and shades. Being tall and slim these lamps were elegant to look at and I had the thought of using them to light each end of a dinner table. The wicks were in fairly good and little used condition.

The problem was to get these lamps into usable condition both as oil lamps with the option of converting these for longer term use as electric lamps instead of storing them away. The glass chimneys were available at a specialist lighting shop for about £5 each, so they were fairly easy to replace. However, the shades that I particularly required were not so easy to get hold of without paying the new price of about £16 each. Luckily, I came across an ugly and cumbersome electrical ceiling light fitting at a car boot sale which happened to have the above shades fitted and the seller was keen to get rid of the whole fitting for £2 only, so as not to take it home again. I did not wish to focus my interest on the shades alone as I feared that the shades in almost brand new condition sold separately would fetch a much higher price, so I purchased the whole unit only to remove the shades and then to dispose of the rest. The final problem was to purchase and fit the adaptors shown in the photo below.

As the power cable can be seen to come out of the side of the burner adaptor it was simply a matter of replacing each unit, with the cable discretely running down the back of the lamp. High efficiency bulbs were fitted and the chimneys and shades were repositioned ready for use. The old burner units were stored safely for re-use/sale in the future as an oil lamp again.

Lamp – Four Branch

The four branch lamp shown above is a creation of mine from a number of separate sources. The (unwired) base which cost me £1 from a charity shop and consisted of a figure and what was a single candle/bulb socket divided (later) by a flat circular brass finished junction box with switch installed. The junction box, a switch and some gold covered 0.5mm2 three core cable were purchased for about £10 from an electrician's suppliers. The four branches with bulb holders attached were stripped from a ceiling candelabra light fitting and purchased for about £2 at a car boot sale. Finally in the central position over the base an arrangement of lamp stem fittings with a loop handle from my scrap box provided a lifting handle.

I had in mind an overall design for my lamp and I now wished that if had two bases so that I could have made a matching pair of lamps.

The key to the construction of the lamp was the junction box. It was necessary to drill suitable sized holes in the circumference of the junction box for the four branches to be assembled, and also a central hole for the switch to be inserted. The main part of the junction box would be fitted via a drilled hole to the base of the box and secured by a nut, allowing the new cable to enter into a junction block via the switch. The lid of the junction box was attached to the decorative candle holder and lifting handle.

With the four branches secured to the junction box with nuts and allowing the wires for each branch to be attached to the junction block the wiring was now completed with an earth wire to the switch, also earthing the whole lamp with a connection to the metal junction box. The lid of the junction box was now fitted bringing the whole lamp together. Candle bulbs and green lampshades completed the lamp following testing.

It is strongly advised that only a qualified or trained person should carry out the rewiring of household items, and where this is not possible, the inspection of the finished item by an electrician is recommended, particularly where the finished goods have exposed metal surfaces.

Lamp Standard

Although unfashionable at this moment, I inherited the above lamp standard and although it needed to be rewired, rubbed down and re-polished it showed considerable workmanship in its design. I had the opportunity to compare it with a modern day 'minimalist' example of a lamp standard which appeared to be little more than a broomstick fitted to a disc.

The lamp required stripping of all electrical fittings prior to rubbing it down with abrasive paper. Fortunately, I was able to rotate the various parts of the lamp standard in a suitable sized lathe which allowed me to apply the abrasive paper evenly over its length. The more intricate parts of the lamp required careful sanding by hand in an easily accessible stationary position. When adequately smoothed down, and dusted off it was time to apply coats of the varnish.

When dry, the bulb holder was re-fitted and the new cable pulled through. A stiff rod or even an opened up wire coat hanger could be used to feed the cable through the two parts of the lamp standard body and the base. A suitable 13A plug was then fitted. With a suitable bulb and shade this lamp was ready for use subject to the inspection of a qualified electrician.

MODELS

Bicycle – Mini to Micro (Ongoing)

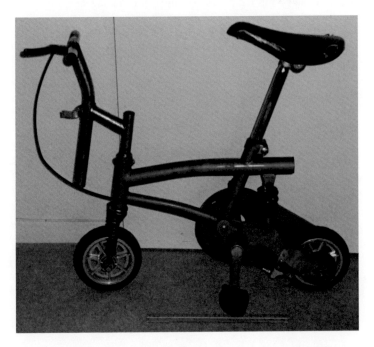

I picked up this tiny bicycle at a car boot sale for about £3 partly because of its quirky nature and also as it reminded me of seeing a much smaller ride-able bicycle in my local cycle shop as a young man. The condition was not very good but it was almost complete and as I intended to use the main parts to construct an even smaller micro-bike it would be adequate for my needs.

After taking some existing measurements I decided to strip the bike down. The wheels and tyres would be usable as they are, along with the chain-wheel set and brake. The chain-guard and the suspension would be discarded.

The frame would need to be reduced in size by as much as possible by removing sections and then rejoining them without the provision for suspension. The 'solid' frame size should become more in proportion with the size of the wheels. The riding position will be maintained by the existing forward setting of the handlebars but new to this design will be the rear setting of the seat. The height of the bottom bracket will need to be maintained at 5 ¼ inches from the ground to allow for the pedals to clear the floor.

The final Micro-Bike has not as yet been completed but is an ongoing project that might as an idea inspire any fellow enthusiasts.

Coracle

This scale model of about 6 inches long caught my interest at a car boot sale. The detail was very impressive, so much so that I felt that I could make a full size coracle without any further reference. The model kept in a clear plastic bag was 50p as it had woodworm, and the bag was to stop it from spreading to other wooden items.

As I had treated other items with woodworm I had a can of chemical treatment left over, and it was easy to coat the affected areas. The bore holes visible after this treatment were carefully filled in with wood stopping, and were no longer easily visible.

I was happy to put this model in my display cabinet with other models. As this was clearly a handmade item possibly sold by a museum shop for perhaps £10 to £25 it was yet another bargain for me that might otherwise have been binned.

Model Steam Roller

I purchased a box of steam related 'toys' and miscellaneous items for £20 at a car boot sale. Most of the contents were incomplete or not working except for a stationary steam engine which I kept along with an (incomplete) steam roller above, and the traction engine over-page. The remainder I sold fetching about £50.

A new driving wheel, coal box and burner tray was required for the steam roller and I was able to obtain these from the maker Mamod at the time for about £10. These parts were easily fitted and apart from some touching in of paintwork and general cleaning up I had a complete working model for about £15, worth about £45 and costing about £100 new. This was a nice addition to my steam toy collection.

Model Steam Traction Engine

As previously mentioned, I purchased a box of steam related 'toys' and miscellaneous items for £20 at a car boot sale. Most of the contents were incomplete or not working except for a stationary steam engine which I kept along with an (incomplete) traction engine above, and the steam roller on the previous page. The remainder I sold on as individual parts fetching about £50.

A new canopy, coal box and burner tray was required for the steam roller and I was able to obtain these from the maker Mamod at the time for about £12. These parts were easily fitted and apart from some touching in of paintwork and general cleaning up I had a complete working model for about £17, worth about £45 and costing about £100 new.

This was a nice addition to my steam toy collection.

GENERAL GOODS

Hoover Vacuum Cleaner

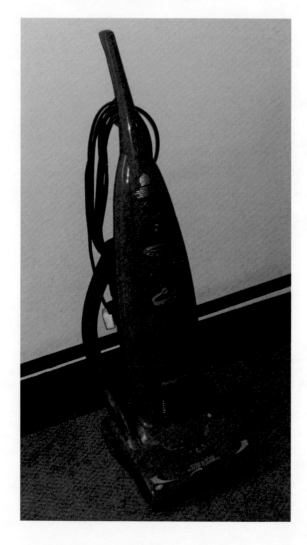

This Hoover was destined for the rubbish tip. It would not always start when switched on, and if the cable was pushed or pulled close to where it entered the body of the machine it would sometimes come on or go off. It was also feared that if the motor was faulty, that the cost of a replacement part would outweigh any costs in having it repaired.

Our cleaner complained that it needed repairing. A call to the Hoover service department by my partner told us that it would cost £70 to just look at it, and a new motor would not be worthwhile as it would be cheaper to buy a new model.

Although this Hoover was about 10 years old it had had little use and I was not happy that it was going to be dumped. This I believed was consumerism at its worst in the lack of affordable solutions to this problem. I also felt it was in the interests of the manufacturers to recommend buying a new model instead of repairing the old one, and this was supported by having such high service costs.

So it was now my turn to get involved with this problem. The most obvious cause to look for was a loose connection in the cleaner.

First it was necessary to remove the covers to gain access to the power connections. We can see in the picture above where the power cable enters from the right into the Hoover via a grommet, then under the cable clamp, and with the outer sheaf cut back the brown and blue wires enter the junction block. Each wire into the junction block was gently pulled in turn, and it proved that all of the connections to be tight as they should be.

The symptoms of the fault could equally be related to a damaged cable. To check this out the logical thing to do was to substitute the potentially damaged power cable (connected to the junction block) with a short piece of similar duty cable that was known to be in satisfactory condition to see if this allowed the Hoover to be switched on and off. The Hoover could now be reliably switched on and off proving that the original power cable was faulty.

A new power cable of the same length and type was purchased along with a 13A plug for about £5. After fitting the new cable the Hoover was given a new lease of life and it continues to work well.

Pipe rack

I tend to buy wooden materials for turning at car boot sales, especially those that have been turned which are often chosen because of the fine grain which gives a good smooth finish.

On this occasion I purchased for about a £1 what appeared to be an inverted mushroom shaped turned item having a stem and a base. The base was hollowed out where the stem entered the base.

The seller had no idea what this was used for and neither did my friends but I believed that it would be a waste to alter the design which was well made, or to take it apart to use the stem and the base separately. Furthermore, it would have been even more of a waste to bin it because I had no use for it.

As a collector of 'smoke-n-alia' I had in the back of my mind that I wanted a continental style of circular pipe rack meant for long stemmed pipes which were currently in danger of being broken. To adapt the current design I would need to use the hollowed base to support the pipe bowls but with a circular disc with holes for the pipe stems to be fitted to the top of the stem giving support to the pipe stems at about the middle of their length, as shown as the finished conversion above.

I was able to find a circular disc of a similar grain and colouring to the base and I set about boring out the holes necessary to fit the central stem, and with 5 equally spaced holes to allow the pipe stems to pass through. The stem fitted to the base was steamed to soften the glue to allow its removal from the base, and then held centrally in a 3 jaw chuck in the lathe so that it could skimmed to produce a close fit to the central hole in the disc. The disc could now be sanded down and varnished to match the base. The whole of the pipe rack could now be assembled, firstly with the stem glued back into the base, and then the disk glued in position at the top of the stem, with the overall finish made good.

The completed pipe rack was a handsome object which I had not previously come across, or been able to purchase before in the UK. The rack was tried out with some long stem pipes in position and they fitted perfectly with the bowls supported in the hollowed base and the long stems supported at about the middle of their length as I would have required.

Although I am now a non-smoker my favourite pipes could now be safely displayed.

Trolley Bag

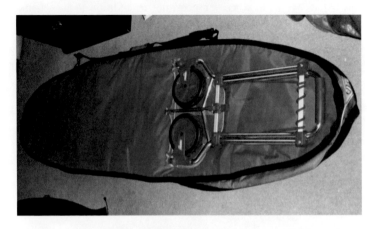

The newly available lightweight aluminium, compact folding trolley with folding wheels which can be purchased at hardware stores for about £25 is a useful item for bargain hunting (at a distance). This trolley opens out to give the equivalent of a traditional sack barrow but for lighter loads. This example deals with making a suitable bag to carry this trolley with you on bargain hunts which to my knowledge is not available to buy.

With no other options that to make my own purpose built trolley bag, I used my lateral thinking skills to consider similar or alternative bags to adapt or modify. I eventually made the bag from what was originally a surfboard bag (see the earlier photo) and cut it down to about a third of its length and using the zipped end for access. As the folded trolley (as seen in the picture) is fairly flat being only a few inches thick, it is not unlike the flat shape of a surf board.

The surfboard bag cost me £4 at a car boot sale and I thought this was a good buy even though it meant a certain amount of cutting and sewing to convert it. The bag, by the way, also happens to be rain and heat resistant.

My new trolley and bag is used when it is not always possible to park close to the car boot sale or flea market. When I decide to buy something I prefer the security of paying in full and taking my goods with me wherever possible. In addition to this, some events are so large and inaccessible that a trolley is the best way to carry some goods. I have in the past, managed to get an outboard motor, and even small pieces of furniture back to the car with ease, when otherwise it would have been a considerable struggle to get the car close enough to load.

It is also possible with the trolley and bag to use public transport in well served areas for bargain hunting. With the finished bag that I have shown I am able to carry it with the strap over one shoulder with little effort. A golf umbrella can also be accommodated in the bag as well as a torch for the keenest of bargain hunters in the early hours of the morning.

The Tumbler

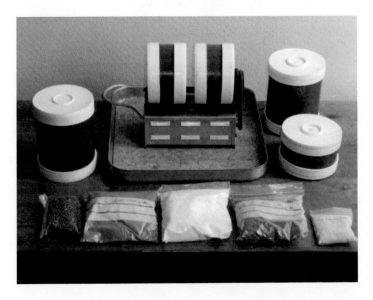

At the time of purchasing this tumbler or barrelling machine some years ago for £6 this was a very popular pastime. In this case the machine itself was complete including 1 long and 2 half-length barrels. These barrels were rotated by rollers in the base driven by a motor which allowed pebbles in an abrasive in each barrel to become polished over a number days.

Part of the appeal as with the fruit press mentioned earlier that could use windfall fruit, is that attractive pebbles found on the beach for free could be polished and mounted in jewellery.

As with many other bargains it is what is damaged or missing that must be considered. The only problem with this purchase was that a number of consumables and spares such as various grades of abrasive powder, drive bands, and so forth were needed at an additional cost. This was not too much of a problem as I was able to find a supplier.

Other uses that I later discovered for this machine was that of tumbling metal detector finds until they were bright and clean. Also in preparing metal for nickel/electro-plating by tumbling components until the abrasive grit or pebbles de-burred and produced a clean matt finish ideal for plating.

An aluminium tray with a cork layer to line the bottom was used to position the tumbling machine so that the tray would contain any of the barrel contents, and the cork to absorb some of the sound of the tumbling often left to run during the night and day.

Sewing Machine

The above picture shows this Victorian sewing machine which cost me about £5 at a car boot sale. The gold decorations on the black paintwork make this an attractive ornament even if unused and kept on a shelf. However, these transfers are worn in places which is to be expected for its age. The sewing machine was in working order except for a bent spindle which carries the needle and can be seen at the top front of the machine. This damage prevented a complete rotation of the winding handle and it was not forced in case of damage being caused, but it was clear that the other parts could be seen to be working.

A new spindle was not likely to be purchased to replace the bent one, and the straightening of the old spindle was not a good idea as if it were not completely true it could cause further damage. However, the damaged part was of a simple design and easy to make. A piece of stock sized (ground and true) silver steel rod would match the spindle diameter exactly but would need to be cut to length with a hacksaw. The design was copied from the damaged spindle and it required a decorative knob at one end and a hole at the other end to hold the shank of the stitching needle. At the side of this hole a small threaded hole was required for a clamping screw to hold the needle in place. A slotted hole was also chain drilled and filed to accept the thread feed arm. Some of these operations would ideally require the use of a small lathe, and a small drilling machine but careful hand skills would also be acceptable. A drill and tap is required for the clamping screw.

The above photo shows the completed spindle fitted into what is now a working sewing machine.

SPORTS RELATED

Creel

This was purchased for £4.95p from a charity shop. It appealed to me as I am interested in fly fishing and the creel somehow is an item that captures my nostalgia for the subject. I do not know if they are still in demand, or if it is possible still to buy these. The creel was in good condition and slightly larger than some that I have come across and with a reasonable size opening in the lid in which to put the fish as they are caught. Also because of its slightly larger size it could be this creel could relate to salmon fishing rather than trout and the like.

The main fault that I could find was that the shoulder strap was missing and to keep in with the traditional nature of this item it was necessary to replace this with good quality leather strap with brass buckle and having a matching shoulder pad that was wider and allowed the strap through it. The leather straps to secure the lid would also need to match the colour tone of the shoulder strap and some coloured shoe polish would help to achieve this.

As with many items purchased at charity shops and car boot sales if there is no damage to the goods requiring repair it is more than likely that a part is missing. In this case the shoulder strap was not too difficult to replace.

Hardy 'Smuggler' fishing rod

The above section of the above 8' fly fishing rod bears the magic name 'Hardy' and is one of 4 pieces of the Smuggler design, now updated by a newer version (starting price at £695). Traditionally, Hardy fly rods were made of split cane but I believe that this one is of carbon fibre and is very light, but not an antique. I paid £35 at a car boot sale for this well used rod and case with little time to examine it in full detail, and expecting to find that all may not be as expected. The picture of the rod and case is shown.

Having later fully assembled the rod, I found that the socket in the top section of the rod might need attention. However, the appeal of this compact rod to me as the name 'Smuggler' implies is that it is ideal for poachers, but in my case small enough to take on holiday.

A novel hinged bamboo cane case came with the rod but I could see that it was intended for a rod with longer sections and the benefits of the compact rod would not be gained. Although I initially intended to shorten the bamboo case I decided that a traditional style canvas based bag with pockets would be lighter and more compact and so I have now acquired one.

As mentioned earlier, there was also some evidence of one or more damaged sockets and what appeared to be professional repairs. Because of this the length of one or more sections is slightly reduced. I was keen to find out whether or not I should be concerned about the possible damage to the rod and I visited a local Hardy stockist.

They had a helpful and experienced member of staff that had worked for The House of Hardy at Alnwick in England who was able to put my mind at rest in that the 'fine action' expected of a Hardy rod was not adversely affected regardless of some "wear and tear". I was also advised that Hardy, through a registration number on the rod, could advise me of the date of purchase (we believed that it was about 30 years old) and possibly some further history, should I require it. I was happy that I had purchased a bargain and did not pursue the matter any further. The rod and bag is shown in the picture below.

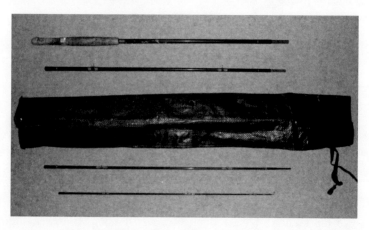

Mountain Bike

This was a project from a number of years ago when a mountain bike mainly consisted of a sturdy frame and wheels, chunky tyres for grip and low ratio gears. Today, we might also want front and rear suspension and disc brakes as well.

However, the bicycle was a part of a rebuild from buying a complete cycle for £12 at a car boot sale. Many good parts were salvaged including some good wheels, chain-wheel and gear changers and brakes. The frame was too small and in bad condition with some dents, so when a good frame without wheels and some other parts was seen at another boot sale I bought it for about £5 being incomplete and unusable as it was.

The new frame was stripped, prepared and re-sprayed in two tone colours. With a new saddle, tyres and tubes and the cleaned and repaired/adjusted gear assembly, the bike was rebuilt as shown above.

The bike has performed well in use and I do not feel tempted to buy a more up to date machine. In particular, I prefer to take my bike (and others) on the back of my car to places more ideal for cycling and on holidays.

Outboard Motor

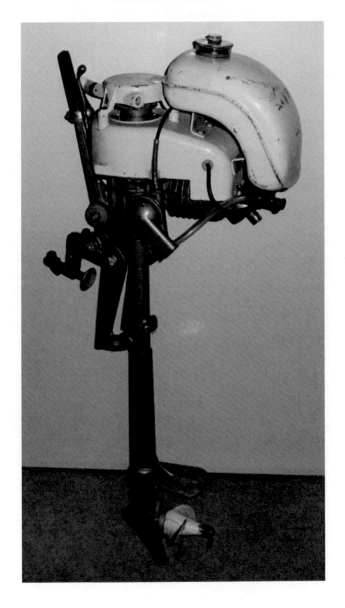

This item came from a car boot sale some time ago and I paid £25 for it. I did not necessarily wish to rebuild this 2 HP two stroke engine but to get it working for my own use with a dinghy.

Having checked the engine over it appeared to be complete but it would not start. It was necessary to go through all of the possible causes and to eliminate them one by one. Firstly, I removed and checked the sparking plug which was not oiled up and was in working order. Next I checked for a spark and this was also satisfactory.

The carburettor was now a suspect for the engine not starting. Fuel was clearly getting through and with the choke on it was allowing a rich mixture to the engine and it could be smelled from the exhaust. The fuel mixture was too rich perhaps, to fire up. I set about taking the carburettor apart and I found that the jet needle was missing.

I decided that this jet needle was essential to get the engine running and that this was the cause of it not starting. I needed to check the internet (with the help of a friend) to purchase a part for an engine that was probably no longer in production and was perhaps 50 years old. Surprisingly, a "Seabee" (the make) owners club existed in Yorkshire and having given a description of the engine a new jet needle was sent to me through the post.

The new part was now fitted and soon the engine fired up.

Rudder for Dinghy

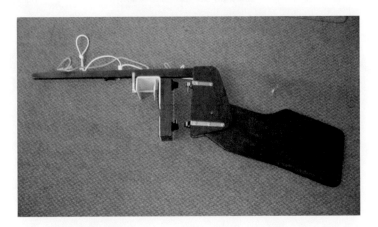

I wanted a rudder on my inflatable dinghy so that I could use it for sailing and rowing. In some waters it was hard to row the dinghy in a straight line, and so far using a paddle from alternate sides for one or two persons has been the only solution, It already has a provision on the transom for attaching an outboard motor but not a pintle and gudgeon as the pivot point for a rudder. So as can be seen above, I have shown a separate bracket (detached but in alignment with the rudder fixings) with a pintle and gudgeon for attaching the rudder and a clamping arrangement for the transom, which I constructed for this purpose.

The rudder shown above (without the bracket) was purchased at a car boot sale for £3. It was in a poor state being badly scuffed and with the blade of the rudder the plywood had started to de-laminate. If I had not bought this item I am sure that it would have been scrapped. Also the mechanism which allowed the blade of the rudder to be raised (in shallow waters) and lowered was not working as the bungee cord also needed replacement.

It was necessary to strip the rudder down completely, firstly to deal with the de-lamination. Here a scalpel was used to clear the gap between the layers of plywood and carefully to push water-proof wood glue into the gap. A stiff piece of material was then positioned over the line of de-lamination and a number of 'G' clamps were clamped along this line to force the layers of ply together until the glue had set. At this point all of the parts of the rudder needed to be sanded smooth and then given about 3 coats of yacht varnish and then allowed to dry.

The rudder was then re-assembled with the cords in place. The position of the rudder blade could now be set for high sand and then deep water by tying loops to hook in place on the rudder steering arm.

I have yet to try the rudder for rowing, and at a later stage to rig up a sail and to try it out as a part of a sailing rig. But I suspect that without the provision for a centre board it may be necessary to fit a substitute for a centre board that can be raised and lowered on each side of the dinghy such as leeboards to prevent drift.

Whelk Pot

I decided to include this as a good example of recycling which I spotted on holiday to the coast. I guess that the size of this container is about 25 to 50 litres. I have come across empty plastic drums like this for containing various liquids for about a £1 if clean, and although we might see these at boot sales and flea markets they are more likely to go straight into a bin or to the rubbish tip.

Although I have not tried to make and use one of these I may well try something similar in the future. A licence may be required for the use of catching shellfish. I believe that some bait is required inside the trap, and that the prey climbs in through the netted opening but is unable to climb out again. This may offer us the reward of a good supper.

SCIENCE RELATED ITEMS

Barometer

This aneroid barometer is Edwardian, made of Oak, and fairly large by comparison with other banjo designs and was overall in good condition. It was purchased at auction for £30 with a broken dial glass which I think held back any further bidding. I happened to have a replacement glass and bezel which had cost me £10 from a car boot sale.

So in the main the old glass and bezel needed to be replaced, but seen here the hand has come lose on its tapered spindle and will need to be re-fitted.

Apart from these works a good polish with clear wax has made this an attractive barometer for the hallway in my house. I shall be able decide what to wear before leaving home and whether or not I need to take a 'brolly' with me.

Clockmakers Lathe

    This tiny lathe, about 5 inches long was bought at a car boot sale for £5. It came in a box that would not stay shut because a part of the catch was missing, and when closed it was not possible to know if it was upside down or not as the box is split equally down the middle, and the lathe rather than being supported could fall out with the other contents. This I believe encouraged the seller to get shot of it. The lathe itself was tatty to say the least, which did not inspire confidence in this precision instrument as to how well it was looked after in the past. Also I do not believe all the lose parts have been saved. However, an item like this in good condition should fetch at least £50 so I believe that this was a good deal. A makers name could add greatly to that price.

    The first task was to repair the box so that the lathe would be protected when restored and that any loose parts would be safely kept together. A new catch was fitted to the box along with handles that would ensure the way up in which the box would be carried and put down. The box was then to be polished after repairs, and a velvet interior lining added to protect the contents.

This small lathe was to be stripped to clean it thoroughly so I used penetrating oil on all of the moving parts so that it could easily be taken apart later on. Each part was removed and any paint, rust and dirt cleaned away. The base (for mounting the lathe) would need to be repainted along with any other painted items, whereas the previously painted headstock and tailstock and any other brass parts would be polished and clear lacquered.

The finished lathe is an attractive item especially because of its tiny size which gives it a novelty value. It also makes one think about the clockmakers skills which are more a thing of the past, except perhaps for odd clock and watch repairers who may now be scarce except for those in the antiques trade.

The Hour Glass(es)

Just as with the magnifying glasses for example, where lens and surrounds can be matched to a variety of designs and materials for handles, these can be very collectable and nice to own. A variety of hour glasses (less frames) are available through a chain of stores and through the internet. It is a matter of taste as to preference to use and/or display of (frameless) hour glasses but I believe that they are too easily broken and they are not a part of traditional design.

The picture below shows some designs of frameless hour glasses.

A very plain and basic hour glass frame needs be little more than 2 wooden discs and three or four pillars. As I am interested in recycling I suggest that these materials can be found at car boot sales and the like, and that more interesting and attractive designs can be made than shown here.

Most antique and collectable hour glasses have frames, some of which may be very ornate. The "hour" glass itself being of a variety of shapes and sizes, with the smaller sizes being for less than an hour, and the larger ones for more than an hour. A 16 inch high glass as shown above (the tallest) measures precisely 2 hours.

In history we may be given to believe that a 15 minute glass may have been used for sermons, and the 30 minute glass for sailors on ships watch, when it would be turned to start again with the next watch. More recently in the lengthy O J Simpson trial in the US the judge used hour glasses to symbolise the time and cost of the lengthy trial.

So should these items appeal, you may wish to "frame" your own glasses if you are able buy them, or even re-frame damaged or plain ones. To do this in its simplest form we need to produce wooden pillars (dowel rods) and end discs to frame the glass. Some more interesting frames have gimbals (as shown below) that allow the glass to be turned within an outer frame. The materials used include a variety of marble, wood, brass, ivory or bone may be used in the more complex and ornate examples.

Traditional hourglasses are shown at the top. They are made more interesting by having turned pillars and end caps. In addition to this inlaid patterns add to the quality of the workmanship and its value. You might wish to make and collect a number of hour glasses of different designs and/or to sell these on as reproductions.

Instrument Cabinet

This type of cabinet is sometimes described as a Toolmaker's cabinet. It is designed to house precision tools and instruments in drawers lined with green felt. However, it can also ideally house small tools (not just for metalwork) and materials for restoration work on wood, ceramics and other materials.

The empty cabinet was found in a country town Saturday flea market along with tools and bric-a-brac. It appeared to be complete including keys, except for a knob missing from one of the drawers. Although the cabinet looked shabby showing considerable wear and tear, the asking price of £90 was on the high side. I was able to haggle, successfully reducing the price to £80, and I remembered that some new cabinets from the USA (at the time) cost in the region of about £350 to £500.

The restoration of the cabinet would require it being stripped down, and to replace later the worn and rusted fittings such as new chromed latches, handle, and corners. New rubber feet, felt drawer linings and the missing knob from a drawer also needed to be replaced. The missing knob was turned on my Unimat 4 lathe out of aluminium to match the dimensions of the other knobs.

The wooden finish on the cabinet and drawers required sanding down and then re-varnishing. Once the varnish had dried the new fittings were fitted. As shown in the photo the restored cabinet looks as though it was in new condition with little or no signs of wear and tear.

The individual drawers allow for tools and materials to be grouped together making even small items easy to find. The drawers can also be removed and taken to wherever you are working with the cabinet left on the bench. And of course the cabinet itself can be taken with you when you may be working away from home.

The top section of the cabinet hinges backwards to allow storage area for personal items such as first aid kits, text books and tables, and even sandwiches.

When not in use any valuables kept within the cabinet can be securely locked firstly by use of the lock in the top lid, which also secures a separate front panel in front covering the drawers or when the top lid is open a separate lock in the cover panel over the drawers can secure the drawers on their own.

Globe – Celestial

This celestial and the following terrestrial globe were acquired from various sources for about £5 each. The globes themselves were of matching sizes in diameter to make them suitable as a pair, but the bases were different so I decided to replace them with matching bases. This globe dated back to the first moon shots in the 1960's and I believe this was a standard NASA design.

The existing dished aluminium base was fitted which I felt to be too lightweight for the globe it supported. I decided on the design shown above which I turned from dark oak, with brass fittings to match for each of the two globes. (See Terrestrial Globe).

It was important to keep the frame of this globe to its original design, with its different axis from that of the Terrestrial Globe, however, a wood screw fixing through the brass cap into the wooden base was the same in each case. Also green felt was glued to the new bases to protect any polished surfaces that they are stood on. As a pair of matched globes they look good either side by side or at either ends of the top of a bookcase and I am pleased to have these in my study.

Globe – Terrestrial

This terrestrial and the previous celestial globes were acquired from various sources for about £5 each. The globes themselves were of matching sizes to make them suitable as a pair, but the bases were of different designs so I decided to replace them with matching bases.

The globe shown above was I believe made in the 1950's showing the political colours of the countries of the earth. Historically, the extensive red shown in the eastern European countries indicates that the globe was made prior to the decline of communist rule.

The existing base was of black plastic which I felt to be too small and lightweight in size for the globe it supported. I decided on the design shown above which I turned from dark oak, with brass fittings to match for each of the two globes.

It was important to keep the frame of this globe to its original design, with its different axis from that of the Terrestrial Globe, however, a wood screw fixing through the brass cap into the wooden base was the same in each case. Also green felt was glued to the new bases to protect any polished surfaces that they are stood on. These globes look good together or at either end of a bookcase.

Magnifying Glass

This magnifying glass is made from separate parts. The glass lens and its brass surround were of good quality but were missing a handle. The "grand" handle shown fitted here was removed from a worn out carving knife blade, making a very attractive match when 'Araldited' together. So both parts now complete bought for a few pounds compare to similar glasses can fetch £25 in the Portobello Road.

Other interesting examples of magnifying glasses as shown above are very collectable and are useful to own. It is possible to use the car boot sales and flea markets to gather suitable lens and potential handles to make your own. The style of handles that can be used can include horn, bone, plastic, brass and wood. The actual design for a handle is unlimited but it must be comfortable to hold, look attractive and it may be quirky.

SCIENTIFIC INSTRUMENTS

Microscope – Brass

The microscope prior to restoration

The microscope above with the makers name of Prior, London is shown before restoration. I purchased this item about 15 years ago at a car boot sale for about £10. We can see most importantly that the viewing lenses are made by Karl Zeiss and are binocular/stereoscopic rather than mono, a sign of an expensive and a good quality microscope. The platform for the specimens to be mounted is unusually large and incomplete. I believe that a glass plate should be slotted into the open platform and could easily be replaced, but this was a good bargaining point for the price paid. Also, I believe that this large open design of the platform may have been used to suit small dissected specimens, (new if allowed) or as I have been told, to examine photographic film. I have also found it useful for examining paper, print, text and especially handwriting.

This Microscope was not a particularly attractive item to have as an ornament on a shelf with the black paint chipped in many places. It would require a new finish. However, the microscope was in usable condition, it is almost completely made of brass which could be exposed and polished, and as previously mentioned it is also has stereoscopic eyepieces made by Karl Zeiss, a very desirable make.

The chipped black paintwork on the microscope would require stripping regardless of whether it would be repainted black, and so the brass finish would be exposed anyway and be considered as the new (lacquered) finish. Although it is desirable to maintain the originality of any restored item I decided that the attractiveness and desirability of the microscope would be greatly enhanced with the polished brass finish, and that this was not uncommon with slightly earlier, 19th Century microscopes.

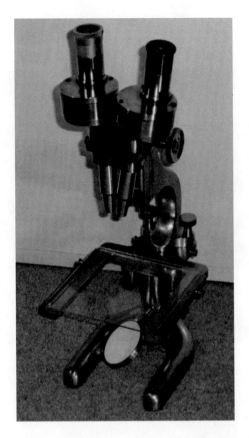

The starting point was carefully to dismantle the microscope into the four main parts being the base, the platform, the upper frame and the lens and focusing system. Care was taken to protect the lenses and to store small screws and the like. Working on each main part in turn starting with the base, a paint stripper was used and the paint was scraped, wire brushed, and the bare surface rubbed down with fine abrasive paper, and finishing off with wire wool and metal polish. The polished brass could then be protected with a clear lacquer.

Care was then taken to re-assemble the whole microscope with a new 2mm thick glass slide for the platform. The two eyepieces were replaced, as original without alteration. The microscope was now set-up/adjusted for use as shown above.

Orrery

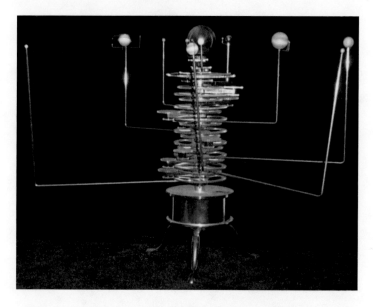

An incomplete and partly built Orrery was purchased from the internet for £75. The parts for this Orrery originally came individually with a weekly magazine relating to astronomy at a cost of a packet of cigarettes each over about nine months. I was luckily able to buy most of the missing parts with back-numbers of the magazine and also from the internet. Having re-arranged parts of the incomplete assembly and fitted the missing parts the Orrery was completed. I believe that if I had not purchased and replaced the missing parts that this Orrery would have been broken and possibly scrapped for its brass value.

The cost was not small but it gave me the opportunity to own a brass Orrery and gain a basic understanding of the related astronomy for about a quarter of the market price. Previously the nearest opportunity for owning an Orrery ranged from cheap plastic toy models for children to expensive antique models for wealthy connoisseurs with nothing affordable for the ordinary enthusiast until now.

The many parts of this Orrery, including the part already assembled, allowed sub-assemblies to be built such as the base with electric drive, while some other parts needed to be assembled when all of the parts were purchased. Guidance notes and a parts list with diagrams assisted with the construction.

As seen in the photo the Orrery can be briefly described as a column of gearwheels with the sun positioned at the top centre. Each geared drive from the central column was fitted with a cranked arm mounted with a planet in line with the level of the sun. The distance of each planet from the sun relates to the scale of the model, as does the amount of speed and rotation in relation to the other planets shown. A small electric motor in the base when switched on will drive the planets around the sun.

Telescope

It can be seen from the close up of the telescope above that some damage has occurred to the brass tubular body of the telescope. In addition to this the part of the viewing lens section that attaches to the tubular body of the telescope has been slightly distorted. Fortunately the lenses remain fully intact and the focusing section of the telescope is fully functional. The dilemma here is that the telescope, although made of brass, it is a cheap reproduction from the far-east, (because of the damage it only cost me £5 to take away) I needed to establish how much time and expense was required to make it look respectable and usable.

Having straightened the tubular body of the telescope as in the photos it was possible to see that it would function as a telescope even without the lenses at each end being in full alignment. The fact that the telescope was usable left me with the challenge of how to go about restoring it.

I had decided that the telescope was not potentially valuable, or of good enough quality, to carry out what I would call a "full or proper restoration" which would involve a new brass tubular body with threaded ends and a newly turned and threaded connector to the viewing lenses.

The cost of the brass materials alone could outweigh the value of an identical reproduction telescope if it were restored as original.

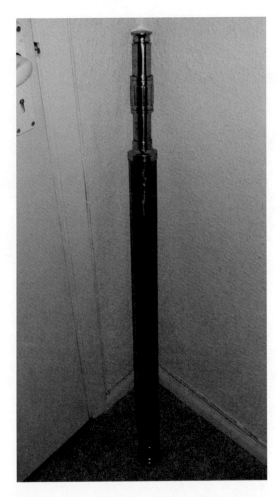

I needed to think laterally to resolve this dilemma. The main problem was to replace the brass tubular body and to make do with the slightly damaged lens connector. Basic attempts to remove the dents in the brass tubular body were not successful. Short of "annealing" the tube by heat treatment, and pulling a close fitting greased hardwood plug through the length of the tube to push out the dents from inside, it would still be unlikely to remove all blemishes. So the tube would need to be replaced by an inexpensive alternative.

The problem with replacing the tubular brass body with another tube was that of the finish. Some brass telescopes can have the tubular body covered in ray skin or leather. My solution is a lightweight tube such as a 2" diameter plastic drainpipe covered in a brown leather effect Fablon which would be rigid enough to ensure the alignment of the lens, and the leather finish would be in keeping with the design. The tube length would also be important to maintain the focal length of the lenses of the telescope.

Overall, the cost of this attractive and usable telescope totalled about £12 in all. It would be ideally mounted to a tripod and positioned to look out at sea or across the countryside.

The Tripod

The legs, made of a hardwood with brass fittings where any adjustments are made, were all covered in dark green paint. It can be seen in the photo above that I have refurbished the brass fittings and the rest were also given the same treatment. The paint was also stripped off the wooden legs and sanded smooth for varnishing with a durable dark brown finish. Once the varnish was dry the whole tripod was re-assembled. The contrast between the dark wood legs and the polished brass made the tripod look very decorative.

The tripod shown was purchased for £5 at a car boot sale. It is very rigid when properly set up and its own weight adds to its stability. I believe that a telescope mounted on this tripod could be left out on a balcony, decking or veranda in reasonable weather conditions without any great concern.

I guess that it may have been used for surveying purposes or suchlike, and it has a professional feel regarding its quality and I believe that it is British made and possibly ex-government property.

A leather strap (screwed to one leg) to hold the folded legs together was also replaced with a good quality new strap in place of the broken one.

At a later stage I would also like to replace the current telescope mount on the tripod which has a "modern" lever operated universal action with a suitable brass mount, possibly of my own design but in keeping with the traditional style.

Overall, the finished tripod has an "antique" appearance with the polished brass and the contrasting dark wood finish. I believe that it would cost perhaps a £100 or more to replace this tripod. The telescope with a brass finish shown previously in this book makes an ideal combination, although if I came across a bigger and better quality telescope it would be useable on this tripod.

Tellurion

Just as with the Orrery shown earlier, I purchased this item from the internet for £95 but this time as a complete but un-assembled kit. The parts for this tellurion originally came individually with a weekly magazine relating to astronomy at a cost of a packet of cigarettes, over about nine months. Unfortunately, this time the weekly parts of the kit had been removed from its packaging and magazine making it extremely difficult to relate the parts to the guidance notes. Again I feel that it was close to being scrapped for its brass value.

With a container of loose parts I needed to label the main parts such as the gearwheels by counting the teeth. Then I needed to relate the many loose screws, gearwheels and body parts to the diagrams until sub-assemblies could be made. The completion of the tellurion soon followed but this was no easy task.

The cost was not small but it gave the opportunity to own a brass tellurion and gain a basic understanding of related astronomy. Previously the nearest opportunity for owning a tellurion was to own a rare antique model normally the preserve of wealthy connoisseurs with nothing affordable for the ordinary enthusiast until now.

As we can see in the photo above this model relates mainly to the relative positions of the Earth, and Moon in rotation around the Sun over a period of time. In particular this relationship between the Earth, the Moon and the Sun has a strong influence over the seas and the tides. As we know the normal the tides occur twice every 24 hour day as the world rotates by one revolution. The epicyclical rotation of the Earth on its axis is responsible, as we may be aware, for the Neap tides which occur every four years and add to the effect of the normal high tides. The position of the Earth in relation to the Moon and the Sun during its various cycles can have the effect of increasing the gravitational pull on the seas as it moves closer to them. The tellurion may indicate, or even forecast, the extreme high tides which may be responsible for flooding.

The seasons of the year will also be shown by the tellurion, and one could argue that climate change over time can also be considered to be a part of this. Extreme heat and excessive flooding can also be linked to the Earth's cycle. Perhaps over many thousands of years this could also support the evolutionary theory of life forms adapting to these climate changes.

Eclipses can also be predicted by the tellurion which can highlight partial and total eclipses. Of course the Earth in the position that we live in will rotate away from the Sun each day to give us night time. The eclipse is in fact easy to understand when the Moon crosses the path of the Earth and blocks out the Sun so we will experience the blacking out of the skies. In some cases an eclipse is looked upon as an important event especially in astronomical terms.

I feel privileged to own this item.

Tropical Sundial with Noon Day Cannon
(Ongoing Project)

The sun dial opposite was designed mainly for tropical climates near the equator where the sun tends to rise directly overhead, and when at noon the sun through the magnifying glass would fire the cannon. The original older versions of these are often valuable antiques and may fetch more than a thousand pounds at auction and are not often seen in the UK. Otherwise, reproductions of this type of sun dial may be seen. I recall seeing small versions of these for sale in the Royal Greenwich Maritime Museum shop for about £125.

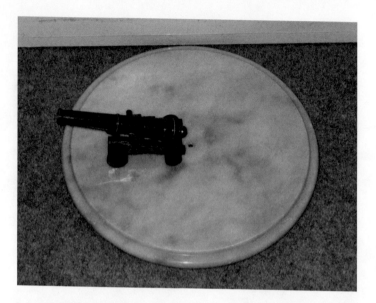

I found this item to be an attractive and interesting timepiece that I would like on display in my house but I do find the likely price to be prohibitive. Just as the theme of my book is to recycle, in doing so we can seek and find parts from boot sales, charity shops and so on, many of which we use to make a complete tropical sundial. The remainder of parts we can attempt to make for ourselves.

In my second photo (an example) you can see a model brass cannon purchased from a charity shop for £4 and a marble base (cheese board or lazy Susan) purchased from a car boot sale for £3. It could be argued that these items contribute at least 50% towards the finished article. Over time, a variety of model cannon and marble bases can be collected and mixed and matched to achieve the ideal scale. A small marble base may be the most suitable for an indoor ornament.

Those of us who enjoy model making/engineering are likely to enjoy the work involved in making this sun dial along with the technical decisions and research required. The cannon itself will need to have been bored out and link to a drilled fuse hole as is normally expected in a real cannon. The "gunpowder" required for firing the cannon would need to be licensed. An alternative called "Pyrobex" is legally available and can be used for the firing of the cannon in the open air instead.

The adjustable magnifying lens holder will require some important metal work to be carried out preferably in brass, along with providing a fixed base to the cannon. A selection of lenses will also be required taking into account a suitable diameter and focal length. Drilling fixing holes through the marble base can be carried out using a "spade" tungsten drill as used with glass, or a new tubular metal design impregnated with diamond. The sun dial markings in hours will also need to be carefully engraved in the marble possibly using a "Dremmel" with a pointed diamond burr and guided by a template. A "gnomon" will need to be fitted in the centre of the base to cast a shadow.

On completion, when you proudly demonstrate the firing of the cannon for the first time you might find that friends may wish to commission you to make them a tropical sun dial from your spare parts gathered during the making of your own dial.

Wimshurst Machine

The item shown above was purchased for £80 from Camden Passage. I was able to reduce the price from £100 by haggling mainly due to a Leyden jar (below) on the left hand rear of the picture being broken. Its age was certainly pre-1950's but not as early as the 1920's, and by its design it was also likely to have been mass produced for education purposes such as school science labs. For me, this was preferable to the many Wimshurst machines made by amateurs using jam jars, although earlier "specialist one offs" made of brass and quality materials could be of great value.

Upon a closer examination all things appeared to be in order except for a lack of a spark which was likely to be caused by a broken Leyden jar which acts as a condenser. This machine is not a valuable antique but a collectible item nonetheless. This helped me to decide whether an identical Leyden jar was required at the cost of perhaps hiring a glassblower, and if not, a matching pair of jars would need to be found as they are not "off the shelf" items. Jam jars have been used for this purpose by amateurs but I would like to keep close to the original design of tall, narrow (slightly tapered) glasses having a thin wall thickness including the bottom.

My closest match to the original design of the Leyden jars has been a pair of clear, tall drinks glasses. These have thin wall thicknesses including the bottoms, although are they are slightly larger in diameter and slightly shorter in height. (As this slight variation could be noticeable it justifies the replacement of the pair of glasses and not just the broken glass). Much of the glass needs to be covered in aluminium foil and I aimed to match the original area covered of about 25 square inches externally, with the same levels matched internally, in both left and right hand jars. Also only about two thirds of the jar heights are covered by foil.

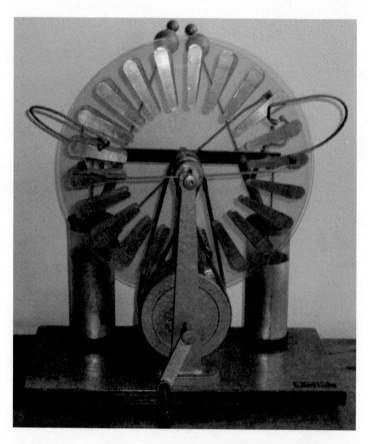

When the Leyden jars were completed (see photos above) it was necessary to adapt the existing connections to each jar. A circuit is required to link the foil inside each jar by a length of chain suspended from the adapted insulated cap on each jar which links with generator via the friction brushes and the contra-rotating wheels. The exterior connection of the jars is through the foil at the base of each jar in contact with an adapted seating on the base board linking the electricity to discharge through the spark across the gap between the two balls. (I understand that 100,000 volts is required to make a jump between the balls set one inch apart). The humidity can affect the ability to create sparks and a lot of tinkering can be required to get the best results.

This machine was originally used to demonstrate the existence of electricity, and later used in experiments such as making dissected frogs legs twitch, as if coming back to life. The Wimshurst Machine is probably best known for its use in Hammer Horror films such as Frankenstein, used along with lightning conductors to bring the monster to life.

The finished Wimshurst Machine is shown on the above page with the new Leyden jars attached.

CONCLUSION

In conclusion, I believe that my examples do show that it is possible to recycle for pleasure and profit. In the main my examples have *been items that have found their way from the oblivion of the* waste mound or incinerator, to being restored and made usable items for my personal pleasure which I intend to keep, but due to the need for storage space I have also sold one or two items at auction for a reasonable profit.

My examples have been purchased from a range sources and I consider that I have gained bargains which in the main after restoration would at least have doubled in value, but we must expect that the demand and value of such goods can vary considerably over time. Only in one or two of the examples such as the corner chair (which was gift) would I have possibly not recovered the expected value of the same item in good condition after the cost of restoration materials.

However, the type of repair, its scale and the likely cost of materials, along with my skill and resources to carry out the work were considered in each case. It is also the fact that some consumables, materials and especially tools purchased for a particular project will be left over and reusable on future projects.

For some types of repairs and general interest use I have invested in some equipment such as a cheap metal arc welder, and a small lathe to extend my scope of work, but I had no intention to link the cost directly to any one particular restoration. For example, the welder made an easy and cheap repair possible with the fruit press and I could easily attribute say 25% of the cost of the £40 welder to this job but I know that in time it will pay for itself as an investment for future projects.

The sources that I have used to purchase the examples shown in this book I would say are approximately 75% car boot sales, about 10% charity shops, and the remainder of 15% to include flea markets, antique fairs and jumble sales.

The prices paid for the examples shown are approximately as given but may have been purchased up to 30 years earlier, and stored until I have been able to carry out a restoration which can affect the apparent price paid. The Brass Microscope for example, was purchased for about £10 some 15 years ago. Today, with inflation we might expect to pay about double this price, and at the time I was lucky to have had a spare £10 in my pocket and to have haggled to reach this price which was probably more than I would have wanted to spend at the time.

I have mentioned earlier in my book in the section on "Planning" that we are not always likely to find items that we need or are specifically searching for at that moment, but that we should have a 'wish list' of projects so that our searches are much more likely to be successful. Fortunately, as with the microscope example above it was on my wish list and I am so glad that I purchased it. I have not seen many similar quality microscopes prior to this opportunity or since.

It is necessary to see beyond the superficial look of our bargain which is at least likely to be dirty and neglected, if not damaged as well. What we need to see is the same item in our minds, which has now been cleaned and polished with any necessary repairs carried out. To some extent this 'vision' may come from the confidence that we have gained from bringing about such a transformation many times before, and for a beginner, the sheer enthusiasm to create the desired results.

As I do not consider myself to be a dealer, the examples were chosen mainly as my personal choice of items to keep rather than for their resale value. This may explain why some of my choices may well be on my "what not to buy list" and I would have expected to buy them more cheaply because of this.

The examples given have shown a range of requirements in terms of parts missing, necessary consumables missing, not being in working order, repairs being required and the need of a general refurbishment. (The lack of necessary consumables as with for example the Tumbler used for pebble polishing, would make this equipment unusable if I was not able to access the necessary abrasive powders). I believe that this gives a realistic expectation of what we can expect of a bargain and that the reader should be aware of such demands on his/her time and money.

For missing parts that are not available for our bargains (or if they were available at retail prices and would be prohibitive) we may need to use lateral thought. There will nearly always be similar parts used for similar functions on other similar equipment or goods. These similar parts, or similar goods, given some careful thought, can nearly always be adapted to work together. Sometimes putting a tricky project like this on hold temporarily, whilst we carry on with another project will allow for new ideas and materials to gather which will resolve matters.

The same use of lateral thought can be used with the adaption of goods for a new purpose. My example of using an Edwardian Oak fire screen frame to hang a gong was a good example of this. The finished Dinner Gong was an attractive and useful adaption, which also filled the market need for quirky items. Unfortunately I was forced to sell this on as a 'marriage' of parts, to recover some space but I would have preferred to keep this.

My examples included two exceptions to the rule, the Mason's coffee pot on its own did not require any restoration but was recycled back to its valued position as a part of tea or dinner service, and it also showed a profit in its sale as a reward for my purchasing what I recognised as a good quality item. The lobster pot was not one of my projects but was observed on a trip to the coast, and I thought that this would not only inspire myself, but also others with this useful design.

I have used a range of skills in carrying out these restorations and I am aware that the "jack of all trades, master of none" saying, but I believe that it is the variety of work that makes things interesting. However, I believe it is more important, to keep "one's hand in" in practising those skills and then to build on them. This simplest of the skills used in many cases was to clean and polish which I am sure is well within the capacity of a beginner or would be craftsmen.

I believe that I have set out some sound guidelines on recycling with this book, which can be followed for the benefit of the individual, and ultimately to society in general.

DISCLAIMER

In the context of my book I wish to stress that honesty is the best policy regarding the reproduction of period items in terms of their age and provenance, and that any repairs whether hidden or not should be declared as a part of the history of the goods. Along with repairs the adaption or marriage of goods, or parts of goods should also be declared. The quality alone of any reproduction items and the workmanship of a restoration should be the main selling point for any goods.

Regarding health and safety, safe working is of prime importance and guards and protective clothing, especially eye protection should be used. Where the safety of any craft process is in question, along with the safety of any finished goods including those for sale to the public, expert advice should be sought. In particular electrical goods should be inspected by a qualified electrician before sale or use.

BIBLIOGRAPHY

A Jackson & D Day *BETTER THAN NEW* BBC 1982

David Dickinson *THE ANTIQUES BUYER* Orion Books Ltd 1999

C Payne & J Gleeson *COLLECTING FURNITURE* Mitchell Beazley 1996

Jeff Wuorio *HOW TO BUY & SELL JUST ABOUT EVERYTHING* Harper Collins Publishers 2003

Lorraine Johnson *HOW TO RESTORE & REPAIR PRACTICALLY EVERYTHING* Walter Parrish International Ltd 1980

Peter Johnson *THE PHILLIPS (Auctioneers) GUIDE TO CHAIRS* Premier Books 1993

M Pooley & J Lomax *REAL CIDER MAKING* Special Interest Model Books Ltd 2009

J & M Miller *ANTIQUES FACT FILE* Mitchell Beazley 1988

P Philip & G Walkling *ANTIQUE FURNITURE EXPERT* Tiger Books International PLC 1999

Tim Wonnacott's *MONEYMAKING ANTIQUES FOR THE FUTURE* Virgin Books Ltd 2004